Watching The
Cow Burn

ASC: Growing up with a Schizophrenic parent

Sigmund Magnusson

BALBOA.PRESS

A DIVISION OF HAY HOUSE

Balboa Press books may be ordered through booksellers or by contacting:

Balboa Press
A Division of Hay House
1663 Liberty Drive
Bloomington, IN 47403
www.balboapress.com
844-682-1282

Cover Image: Evgovorov

Print information available on the last page.

ISBN: 979-8-7652-5530-8 (sc)
ISBN: 979-8-7652-5574-2 (hc)
ISBN: 979-8-7652-5529-2 (e)

Library of Congress Control Number: 2024918455

Balboa Press rev. date: 09/12/2024

What are the things that make you what you are, you? Experts tell us that there are many things which lend themselves to the formation of a person's personality. It is often debated that nature is the more dominant factor governing personality while others contend it is the nurturing aspect of humanity that makes us what we are.

In the case of nature, genetics is the key player producing personality. It's just a matter of which nucleotides are connected driving and dictating which proteins are synthesized and like magic you become you the day you are born.

In the other camp, nurture says that you are shaped and molded by your environment. That is to say, every experience you have from the time you are born sculpts and molds you into who you are. So, the babysitter you had, the dog you lost, scolding and beating with a two by four for marking on the walls go into forming your personality. However, most of us likely realize the truth of how personality forms lie somewhere in the middle.

In basic psychology, students are taught a lesson about an experiment in primate behavior. Capuchin baby monkeys are given a bottle for feeding with either a wire imitation mother or with a soft furry imitation mother. Invariably, when given the option, the babies chose the soft furry mother. If the babies are not given the option and only have the wire imitation mother the babies become frail and malnourished. This would be an example of our nature requiring a certain sort of nurturing. All primates prefer warmth and softness to something that is cold and unyielding. After all, would you prefer a cold, hard and rigid parent?

What I will try to do is provide insight into the life experiences of a young man and how events in his life shaped his character. What follows are life experiences, perceptions, fears, etc. This story is complicated by the mental illness of his Father. His Father was diagnosed as a Homicidal Paranoid Schizophrenic. Schizophrenia even at this time in late 2024 is still not well understood. It is not a disease of split or multiple personalities as was the character "Cybil". Scientists believe schizophrenia is caused by an excess amount of dopamine being present in the brain. The excess of dopamine can cause anxiety, irritability, delusional mentation and hallucinations.

Hallucinations can come in different forms. They can be auditory in nature where hearing voices that aren't real is experienced. They may also be visual which is not uncommon where people and things are seen that are not there.

In many cases, while the person is hallucinating, they can often still communicate with a person in the "outside world". The individual hallucinating might be talking to their dead Aunt Lucille and you can ask them a question and they will often respond. Sometimes appropriately and sometimes not.

However, visual hallucinations are especially troublesome because it's almost as though they are experiencing virtual reality. They believe their hallucination is real and it may be very difficult if not impossible for you to get their attention. It may take physical contact such as light touching or as severe as grabbing, pulling or even tackling to get their attention. Sometimes, there is no getting through to them at all. So, if you need some information, an item, a ride to school, lunch money or something else you might have better luck with a total stranger.

As with all mental illnesses there is no cure for schizophrenia. There are only therapies and treatments such as shock therapy, music therapy, recreational therapy and drug therapy which has promise but is far from perfect.

As with all mental illnesses there is no cure for schizophrenia, only partially effective treatment. Therapies range from treatments such as shock therapy, music therapy, recreational therapy and of course drug therapy. Drug therapies have improved over the years, but not nearly the pace of the ground that has been made in areas such as gastroenterology or cardiology.

There are a multitude of reasons for this such as, funding for research, ethical considerations, and overall societal priority. After all, more people die from heart attacks and cancer than from mental illness. But you would never know that from all media reports concerning mass shootings and the connected mental illness which is somehow not adequately connected by the media. Again, with the desensitization and growing disconnectedness in our society if you aren't directly affected by something it just doesn't matter that much. Public apathy and indifference are the most fundamental of all reasons as to why greater strides in research have not been made regarding mental illness. No one really cares unless someone is shot or killed by someone mentally ill and then it's only a news flash and quickly forgotten.

As of 2014 it was estimated that about 2.6 million people in the U.S. were diagnosed with schizophrenia. This number is roughly five times higher than the number of people diagnosed with multiple sclerosis. The direct annual cost of schizophrenia to the federal government and states is about $20 billion dollars. The total burden of schizophrenia on the U.S. economy is estimated between $32 and $65 billion annually. The emotional cost, social cost, and psychological stress placed on family and friends of schizophrenics can never be measured or paid and that is what is most stressed by the disease as well as the life and future of the schizophrenic.

The truth is our mental health care system is in shambles and has not improved much since the time of my childhood in the 1970s and 1980s.

I have worked in healthcare for over 20 years and I've seen overcrowding in psych wards, patients waiting for days or even weeks to get placed in a psych facility.

There simply are too many patients with psychiatric issues or emotional health issues and just not nearly enough providers due to underfunding at the Federal level and extremely poor to non-existent reimbursement for Psychiatrists or Psychologists.

While Congressional leaders cry foul about second amendment rights, planned parenthood/abortion rights, LGTBQ rights or any other rights. They do little to nothing to stem the tide of mentally ill patients who show up to medical treatment facilities everyday only to be turned away because they do not have a psychologist/psychiatrist on staff due to lack of funding.

CHAPTER 1

The Early Years

My first memories from childhood are memories such as playing in my crib with toys and stuffed animals while my mother worked, memories of potty training and missing the mark, memories of sitting on the patio or our country home on the family farm with a dog twice my size that was a wolf hybrid. Things that any child might recall from their early years.

I grew up with two older sisters and an older brother. My father farmed the family farm and my mother was a schoolteacher. It sounds All American, doesn't it? And for the most part, it really was. My father was given custodial duties of the family farm when my grandfather passed away. Neither of my two aunts nor my grandmother were about to get on the tractor, hook up the plow and start plowing the farmland. That was just not a womanly or matriarchal thing to do back in the 1960s. Even with the sexual revolution roaring on the coasts, as is now, sexual and gender roles were different on the farm and nearby cities just as they are somewhat today. In any event, my father was tasked with maintaining the family farm "estate".

The usual farm hours were kept. You know, sunup to sundown. We had the suitable crops for our region; wheat, milo, hay, corn, etc. There were also a few dozen head of white face short horn cattle and chickens too. Our drinking water was supplied by a well that was about a hundred years old. Thanks be to God we had electricity, otherwise summers could have been overwhelming. We did not have central air but did have a couple of window units. Central air was just too expensive.

The house we lived in, on this farm, was built sometime in the 1940s. It was a one-story house with three large bedrooms. One bedroom was a wall of windows facing north that was unbearable in the summer; however, in the wintertime when cold weather would occur that wall of windows could very well be the only tolerable room in the house aside from the den which had a black iron wood burning stove.

The house had a large open country kitchen that was large enough to park a couple of cars. For heat in the winter we would huddle around the black iron stove in our den and would try to pick up a signal on the T.V. by adjusting the rabbit ears to pick up that signal 30 miles away in Kansas.

When you are shivering, and the house temp is 50 degrees that adds a factor of difficulty in trying to adjust those rabbit ears to pick up the signal. For you Northerners that internal house temperature may not seem like much but for a little kid living in the South it was cold.

People often have a misconception about the weather in my home state, especially Yankees. People who don't live here don't realize how quickly the temperature can drop. I've witnessed rapid temperature drops of 40 degrees or more in a matter of seconds while working on the farm as a teenager. For instance, in the time it takes for an individual to walk from his front door to get the paper and return inside the temperature could drop from 70 degrees Fahrenheit to 30 degrees Fahrenheit.

Imagine if you are working on a farm 300 or 400 feet away from your truck while you are cutting down trees and stacking wood. The weather could get really uncomfortable really fast and you might not be prepared. For Bums in the Kansas City area, it could mean death from exposure. No joke.

The main source of income on the farm was my mother's once a month paycheck from being a schoolteacher. When her paycheck came that meant we could actually eat. We could go to the grocery store and buy food. It may not seem like much but if you have ever been poor, you get it.

To most people a trip to the grocery store is pedantic, boring, tedious, etc. However, for a child that has been eating nothing but beef heart and kidneys a trip to the grocery store could be exhilarating.

I'm sure it makes you want to cry. A family eating steak, hamburgers, and the like has nothing to complain about. After all, there are always starving kids somewhere in the world. I should be so thankful to be blessed with beef in all its varieties. I'm sure Dr. Atkins would have highly endorsed my family's diet. Remember this though, when you eat steak every day, day in and out, eventually you will get tired of it. My mother was a wonderful cook and inventive, but there are only so many ways to prepare and serve beef. Honestly, for about four years after I left my house while I was in the Marine Corps, I avoided beef as often as possible. I did not try a filet mignon until in my thirties.

My father's income was erratic. It's not that my father didn't try to provide income, it's just that the nature of farm life is seasonal and sometimes like nature unpredictable. My father would plow not only our farm but other people's land for additional money when he possibly could. When the planting and harvesting was over that was the end of farming income for the season. Not much money for a while. per Mom and Dad, except for selling a bull or heifer at the Stockyards or slaughterhouse. My father worked long hours and he worked hard hours. If it wasn't plowing that had to be done, there was feeding the cattle, mending fences and a multitude of other tasks mostly dealing with farm equipment to occupy his time. There was no money to made in the repairs, but I have no doubt hundreds if not thousands of dollars were saved by his regular maintenance of farm equipment. As any farmer routinerepairs of equipment are just part of the occupation.

I'm sure my father felt like he had been given a gift from God when my older brother was born. Or did he? I no doubt remember my brother, who is more than 10 years older than me, helping our father out by plowing the pasture, breaking rocks, digging post holes, feeding, and watering the cows and similar tasks. He was a free farm hand after all. That's how it should be with a son. Right?

We had a tenant who paid to stay on the land in his travel trailer. This was not uncommon and still is a somewhat common practice for landowners. Mr. Thompson the tenant, would often assist my father with menial tasks. I did not visit the trailer to often due to being too little. However, when I got older, I would sneak out with my older brother William to visit Mr. Thompson.

Mr. Thompson was a friendly man. He was always ready to invite you in and eager to talk. He had a lot of southwestern paraphernalia, such as large belt buckles, snakeskin belts, assorted cowboy hats and ropes. This was all very cool stuff to a little five-year-old boy. He was the closest thing to a cowboy that I had ever seen. The man seemed very cool. After all, when I watched the Lone Ranger, I thought of Mr. Thompson.

William being more than 10 years older than me was naturally attracted to this man. After all, he was another male role model and if Will wanted a beer, it was his to have, so long as our Dad never found out.

Who was I to tell my 16-year-old brother what he should be doing? I didn't even know what I should be doing. I mean, I knew I wasn't supposed to tell lies, hit my siblings, or drink liquid plumber, but beer and alcohol was way beyond me. Don't misunderstand. My brother had friends of his own age who had ways of getting beer, but Mr. Thompson was only a hundred yards away and the closest neighbor was a mile down the road. I'm sure that on certain nights when Mr. Thompson was in his own trailer Will looked forward to having a cold one. This happened rarely but it did happen often enough for this five-year-old to remember.

I honestly think our mother was oblivious. My father; however, I'm not too sure about. He might have been oblivious as well. Neither he nor my mother ever drank an ounce of alcohol and certainly not even at communion. My mother and father may have seen Will's visits to Mr.

Thompson as innocent jaw jacking. I'm sure it was a outlet for Will who did not have any other such outlet under our father's strict hand.

My sisters being sisters were and are quite different from Will and I. Amanda is a year older than Will and she always let him know it and any other way in which she had the upper hand William would find out whether he wanted to or not.

Amanda was one of the popular girls at high school. She had looks. She's fairly intelligent but by no means was her intellect her ticket to popularity. She was attractive and that was it. You know how it works. An attractive girl has a few friends. She is then dated by a few popular boys and soon she is one of the most popular girls in the school, or something like that.

My brother played football in high school for a couple of years and was good enough to be a starter on Junior Varsity as a freshman. He was pretty popular because of his talent on the grid iron. However, William's popularity was short lived because he developed acne so bad that a dermatologist told our parents he could not play any more due to potentially becoming septic due to the acne. So, Will had to quit and there went his outlet from the farm aside from Mr. Thompson.

This devastated Will. He had just lost any means to popularity. In other words, he'd lost any avenue into acceptance by his peers. Though he did still participate in F.F.A which was good for him.

Amanda, being the merciful sister, she was, found a way to make fun of her brother's plight. She would say things to him such as "Shut up crater face or say you can't even play football" in front of their mutual friends. Of course, there were other variations she called him such as zit head, pus boy and acne man.

Imagine the impact this would have on a teenage boy who just recently lost his means to popularity and success. I can remember day after day Will taking 20-30 minutes underneath a heat lamp as therapy to rid him of the acne. This of course was unsuccessful. This was pre-Accutane.

I never remember my brother crying about his situation, but I would not have blamed him if he had. Not only was his beloved sister making fun of him but now all of his supposed friends thought it was cool because his super cool older sister Miss popularity queen set the precedent to mock my brother. It's a wonder there wasn't a Columbine 20 years earlier.

Will's solution to his predicament was to find a new set of friends. Could anyone blame him? He became more involved in F.F.A. and high school engine mechanics (A.K.A shop) He found a lot of similar people in those organizations. He made the adjustment.

Rarely is someone in the Ag program ever going to be a popular person school wide. Especially at a high school like the one Amanda and Will attended. Both of them were part of graduating classes numbering over 500 in the late 1970s.

Will was also old enough to get a job after his last year in football. He was already 16 and able to drive. His birthday was early in the school year and because of his interest in mechanics he was able to restore a 1960's model Chevrolet pickup that had been sitting around on the family farm since our grandfather's death 10 years prior. He used this car to get a job during the winter. This was okay with Dad only because it didn't conflict with plowing or harvesting. But if there were chores to do then by God, Will was going to do them, whether he was tired or not.

Will got a job at a local shopping store and he took the late shift as could be expected for a teenager that is still in school. He worked 30 hours a week and made enough money to buy himself a few things and pay for gas when gas was available. Do you remember the late 1970's.

I'm sure this gave him some sense of empowerment. He now had his own truck, his own job, and his own money. Everything a teenage boy could want. Except he didn't have a girlfriend, but man did he want one.

Amanda had her thing going too. Being a year older than Will, she had her job, her car and her money. There were differences though. Amanda's car was practically brand new and our parents helped Amanda buy it. She did pay for her own gas but beyond that it was her free ride to school, extra curricular activities, hang outs, and her part time job at America's largest Hamburger joint, at the time. She also had tons of guys hanging around her. After all she was pretty and popular.

Every once and a while Amanda would bring home a boyfriend. This would really irritate our father. It wasn't like it was unexpected though. Amanda would come home around five o'clock or so and say, "Daddy and or Mom, by the way, Frank will be over in 30 minutes or so". Our Mom had no problem with this. She just had to throw some extra beef in the oven. No big deal since we always had some on hand.

Our father on the other hand had a very different take on things. If you were a visitor to the Magnusson family farm and you were a teenage boy there to visit my father's teenage baby girl: you might be a little surprised. After ringing the doorbell, the door would open and you would see my father standing in the front door greeting with a loaded 12-gauge shotgun.

No shit!!

My father was not a scary man, but he could be intimidating. He was little over average height at five feet and eleven inches and about 190 lbs. in his late thirties and early forties. He was muscular and he had hard Germanic features. Top this off with a 12-gauge shotgun loaded shotgun and you might see a few lighter hearted teenage boys run to their car and drive down the long gravel road from our farmhouse as fast as they could. In plain English, these boys were scared shitless. I remember my Dad celebrating a few times when the boys would scamper away. We would all laugh about it. All of us except poor little Amanda., but she knew better than to argue with our father. Free speech was not a ratified amendment on the Magnusson farm; at least not for children anyway.

Eventually Amanda was able to find two or three boys who were brave enough to state their "honorable" intention. One of them actually ended up marrying her then divorcing her and then remarrying her.

When Amanda was eighteen and close to graduating, she had decided she had enough of life on the Magnusson farm She and her boyfriend

Robert, who was twenty decided to elope or at least halfway eloped. It turns out all of Robert's family was at the wedding but the rest of the Magnusson family, was conspicuously missing.

The loaded shotgun must have done the trick. Although, it seemed odd even to a six-year-old that his big sister who helped watch over him and said so many times how she loved him didn't invite him or anybody else he knew and loved to her special occasion.

CHAPTER 2

Now that Amanda was away and married and Will was becoming more independent of the family my interactions with my other sister increased. This sister was closest to me in age and of all of my siblings looks most similar to me. Except of course she is a few inches shorter, lighter, and attractive as one may expect for a female.

Emily always had a serious chip on her shoulder. She had to compete with Amanda for attention. Not an easy thing for a sister seven years younger than her older sister. I have little knowledge pf the competition between them at three and ten years of age, but I remember vividly the arguments, shouting matches, and cat fights that would occur between the eleven and eighteen-year-old girls. Of course, it did not help that they had to share rooms. How many families have enough rooms for each child to have their own?

Oh, the arguments! Amanda would yell to mom," Emily's ruining all of my clothes. Emily's ruining all my make-up, Emily's ruining my life, "wha, wha, wha". Of course; our mother would have to tell Emily to cease and desist before our father got home or someone would get a whipping.

I have no doubt that when Amanda eloped that Emily was overjoyed. And it wasn't because of her sister's newfound happiness either. Emily now had her own room, her own closet, her own phone, etc. What more could a girl in the throes of puberty want plus that she was rid of her tormentor, Amanda.

Emily did not have an easy infancy or toddler hood. She was born a good length and weight at the time of her birth. She received a good Apgar score when she was born, sometime between 6 months and 14 months of age Emily came down with an ear infection which caused her temporary deafness or at the very least severely hearing impaired.

Emily was a bright and curious child by all accounts. She started walking at 9 months of age and from then on, she kept our parent's hands full. She was one of those children that regardless of how many times you told her no, scolded her, or even spanked her; if she had her mind made up she was going to do what she had in mind unless you forcefully removed her from the situation or area. Emily's hearing impairment did not help matters. It delayed her speech until she was nearly four which is very unusual for girls. Luckily for her and our parents her hearing did return to her. However, I can attest that she is tone deaf as she cannot match a pitch to save her life.

Emily's relationship with Will was a defacto relationship. Will viewed Emily as his little sister but he did not want that responsibility. He distanced himself as much as possible. Will did his big brotherly duties such as picking up Emily from school or dropping her off to drama club occasionally, but it was only cause he had to do it. Emily is by nature a contrarian and always wants to argue. Will did not appreciate this and would rather avoid the interaction if he could. So, he avoided Emily whenever possible. Being the little brother, I was easy prey for Emily. Of Emily wanted to do something I pretty much was obliged to go along with it. Whatever it was.

Will had a big F.F.A project in his junior year in high school. He had to raise and sell the chickens as well as successfully breed the chickens. At one time during this project, we must have had over 400 Rhode Island Reds in our barn. It was in the barn that I witnessed the cruelty of Mother Nature.

The pecking order is Mother Nature in synopsis. To see chickens peck each other to death is not uncommon but it did leave a lasting impression upon my six-year-old eyes. It is well known that chickens eat not only seeds, bugs and toads but each other as well. Yes, they are cannibals.

It did not make sense to me that a small chick should be pecked to death by its larger members of the flock, but this did happen often enough. My father and brother would sometimes try and intervene but were often unsuccessful as usually the chicks were dead or too far gone when my brother would remove them. Besides my dad and brother had far more things to do other than tend to a few hundred chickens all day long.

Although, not as severe as a pecking order of the chickens; the pecking order of the Magnusson household was in effect at all times when mom and dad were not watching. So, if Emily wanted me to play dress up and mom and dad were not around, guess who got to play dress up as the opposite sex. Just strange I think that any sister would do this to her brother.

It didn't help me that I had teethed on her hair as a toddler. I was five years younger. It didn't help either that I had teethed on her hair as a toddler. I was five years younger. It also didn't help that as a three-year-old toddler I had hit her with a Kirby vacuum attachment. I paid for that with a stern whipping. I never touched my sister again in a forceful way again, playful or not from that day forward. I had become my sister's plaything.

My father's send of punishment wasn't exactly fair. Sexual discrimination was if full effect. If you were a son you got the beating; if you were a daughter a tongue lashing and maybe a slap on the wrist, literally. One time in particular, when I was about five, Will and I were playing around on a Saturday morning as brothers do. Will slipped backward and in doing so accidentally kicked me in the eye. Being the five-year-old I was I had to go and tell someone or anyone about it.

In my whiny five-year-old voice I said," Will kicked me in the eye". Unfortunately for Will, my father was in earshot. My father flew into our room so fast you would have though he was The Flash©. He immediately hit Will in the chest with his entire body and sent Will careening across the room. My Father said something to the effect of "This will teach you to pick on someone your own size". My father obviously felt that alone was not enough. He hit my brother in the head and gut a few times for good measure.

All Will could do was crawl into a fetal position for protection. Eventually, after a few minutes our father had decided he'd had enough. Will staggered around the room and made it to his bed and gave me a look I will never forget. From that day forward, I never again told my parents a word of what my brother was planning or doing.

There were many times when I was growing up that I could help Will with certain things or errands that Will had no business doing. There were many times I should have said something, but I was bound by shear guilt to remain quiet. I had already witnessed what could happen if our father found out. Besides, who, was Will hurting anyway?

Things were pretty peaceful in the household after Amanda's elopement. Emily had her way exploiting her younger brother. Will was busy helping our father and had just started his first job. Our mother was busy finishing up her papers to earn her master's degree and things were moving along at a peaceful pace.

That year I began first grade in public school. Emily began junior high school. Will was in his senior year at the local high school. It was to be an eventful year.

It so happened at the school my mother taught at there was another teacher with a son my age. We immediately became best friends and played together every day after school. We did homework together. That's right we had homework in the first grade. We remained best friends throughout high school, from elementary through high school.

It was a great relief for me to have a friend. Someone I could do something with outside of the family. After all, at home was our closest neighbor who was a mild away. None of our neighbors had any children my age. Whenever Thomas and I met after school we had a great time.

Emily found out that she was pretty smart that year. Every report card that she brought home had nothing but straight A's. Emily was very proud of her report cards. I suspect the main reason for this was that neither Will nor Amanda had done this before. They did have good graded please don't misunderstand. But they never had made straight A's before, report card after report card. Especially, not with the one teacher Emily had for history. Neither Will nor Amanda had managed to get A's in this man's class, but Emily had done it. She had made A's for all other classes as well.

Emily had done it right. She had done it the hard way. Every day after school, as soon as we would get home she would go directly to her room, turn on her light, close the door and study.

She did this for hours on end. She would come out for dinner, but she kept interaction to a minimum until she went to bed. There were a few times when she would refuse to come to dinner for whatever reason. That did not fly well when our father was around because our father would immediately grab her by the hand and bring her to the table by force.

This behavior of Emily's continued through junior high and high school. She found her way into the niche of intellectuals or in high school or in high school terms "The Nerds". She was in German club, debate and speech.

Emily was quite popular in her circle of friends. But as is with the nature of people such as Emily, she became more reclusive at home. Her interaction with me at home became less and less over the years.

On one hand, I was grateful, I was not being tormented by my older sister any longer. On the other hand, I did miss talking and playing with her with the regularity that we did. But after all, that is the nature of growing up.

Emily did occasionally date in high school. She was an attractive girl, but she was not about to let someone, or something get in her way of going to college and getting out of Kansas.

Emily walked the straight and narrow path through high school. She did what her teachers advised. She did well on her S.A.T.s and in her senior year she was the proud recipient of a Presidential scholarship to Wichita State.

For the benefit of you Yankees, Kansas is a large state. A trip from Kansas City to Wichita is about the same as traveling from Upstate New York to Washington D.C. So, with her acceptance letter and admission into Wichita State, Emily gleefully left the Magnusson household and was a long distance from all of the Magnusson problems, for a while anyway.

CHAPTER 3

It's time you find out a little about me. My full name is Michael Sigmund Magnusson. I was born April 1, 1972, to my parents Michael and Marie Magnusson. My mother always said I was a well-behaved baby and child. When she needed me to be quiet, so that she could study for graduate school, she would just put me in my crib or playpen, and I would play quietly for hours on end.

This often made me wonder if I truly was intent and content to play for hours on end or maybe I just gave up after a while and became conditioned to just go in the crib or playpen. No infant or child, my own, or other children I have come across are so willing to go into a crib or playpen and play for hours on end without a fuss.

I'm not inferring that I may have been neglected because I had more than enough interaction with my brothers and sisters. I just think my mother may have had a bit too much on her plate.

Who knows, maybe it is possible that an infant can be so in tune with its mother's emotional state on a day in day out basis that he knows how to behave. I've heard this sort of thing happening in fight or flight situations but not in the home on a regular basis. However, I can tell you that as far back as I can remember I have always had sympathy for individuals in difficult situations and I still do to this day.

When I was about four years of age the U.S. government bought a parcel of our family's land. I remember the large earthmoving equipment and the constant presence the construction crews had until the piece of road work was finished for the completion of a highway to connect two majorinterstates together.

The U.S. government paid my family for the purchase of 60 acres. The payment was around $ 10,000 or so I heard. This payment began a squabble between my father and his two sisters that last until my father's death and remained at the time of the initial writing of this account.

My Aunt Laura was relentless. According to my father and his older sister Inge, their sister Laura had received her fair share. Laura, being the squeaky wheel that she was, complained she didn't receive her fair share and complained to her mother Zelda. My grandmother, in all her wisdom, forked over more money to get Aunt Laura to be quiet. This act created a dispute between my father and grandmother over my grandfather's will that only was settled around the time of my father's death.

My grandmother confided in me one day when I was visiting her that she had felt guilty about the way Laura had been raised. My grandmother felt that when they moved from their house in the country when Laura was a teenager that it had upset her growth and she had never been stable since. My grandmother could not imagine where and how she had gone wrong with Laura. Nevertheless, the damage was done. I was 28 when my grandmother told me this. My father had died the previous years when I was 27 years of age.

I can only imagine the reason my grandmother told me this was somehow for forgiveness, absolution or understanding. She knew I was not a Priest or Clergy. I still to this day am unsure of how I feel towards Aunt Laura. She was the source of so many arguments between my mother and father. On more than one occasion plates were broken over that miserable human being.

The odd thing to me, was that at the age of 10, I was forced to make the same change moving from the country to suburbs as Aunt Laura had done so many years prior. Unlike her, I adjusted without a problem. However, I do not have the personality disorder that I believe Aunt Laura has.

I have few memories of Aunt Laura as a child. She was never around. She never came by at Thanksgiving, Christmas, Easter or any Sunday or some other given Sunday or Holiday. The only time I ever saw her was when she came by to contest affairs of money and how was she getting along. Laura had the uncanny ability to give my family and her sister's family nothing, but trouble and she had so much favor with my grandmother that my Aunt Inge's family and my father often speculated Laura was not my grandfather's child.

My grandfather Magnusson was a pharmacist and a farmer. He had inherited the Magnusson farm after his father and mother's passing. He was torn between two competing and demanding occupations.

He worked 50-60 hours a week and due to his work schedule, he had little time to work on the farm except early in the morning, late in the evening and on the weekends. Due to the lack of time my grandfather had to spend on farm tending to cattle and crops he had to hire a farmhand/handyman. It has been said that Aunt Laura had an uncanny resemblance to this hired farmhand. I'm sure that" secret" will travel with my mother to her grave.

I started preschool at 4 years of age. This is not uncommon, but I believe this just demonstrates my mother's commitment to education and its value. My mother was not only a teacher but was a specialist in early childhood education.

I remember preschool as a pleasant experience where I made friends and learned with other children my age. I leaned my numbers, alphabet and how to read a few single syllable words. Kindergarten was more of the same.

It wasn't until public school and first grade that I met my friend for the next twelve years, Thomas. As I stated before we did nearly everything together. We played football together, worked together, double dated together and played in band together. We were pretty close.

I remember pretty much all of my elementary experience as pleasant and constructive. My teachers we're not cruel or mean, most of them anyway. Most were in fact nurturing and fair. I was and my fellow students were fortunate in that regard. I was also fortunate enough to be in a school system that was completely racially integrated and financially sound. There was little, if any racism, that was overt.

There were however, two distinct experiences in elementary school that forever colored my perspective on my family and school. The first incident happened when I was about eight years of age. My mother had planned that over spring break we were going to go up to Oklahoma to visit relatives. My mom had rented a car that Monday and we were to head up that day.

My sister Emily and I were eager to go up with our brother to see relatives we had not seen or in my case meet relatives I had never met. My father was staying back to tend to livestock and crops.

My sister and I had been lollygagging about getting in the car. My father did not care for our lollygagging and decided he would grab a peach tree switch and teach us a lesson. As Emily and I were about to grab our bags my father lit into both of us. He first began lashing me in the chest. Then he lashed Emily as she turned around. As she tried to get away, he grabbed her and threw her against the wall. My father then began lashing both of us. As we cried and pleaded for him to stop, he did not relent. As the lashing continued Emily gallantly threw me in front of her to use me as a shield from my father and his peach tree switch. This was effective for her as now I was taking the full brunt of my father's rage. He continued for at least another thirty seconds, but it seemed to last forever while it was happening.

Emily and I were never so glad as when we were in that car. When we told my mother about what had happened, she was surprised but not shocked. When I told my mom, what had happened and how Emily used me to block my father's lashes. My mother said Emily was just trying to protect me. That's really a stretch even to an eight-year-old. Oh my God, she did not hear a word I had just said, or did she?

We had a great time with my relatives in Oklahoma. I didn't want to go back to school; for more than one reason. I had a wonderful time playing with my cousins and on their farm. I also still had marks on my body from the lashing I received from my father. I prayed when I got to school no one would notice. I wore long sleeve shirts and my usual blue jeans for the week. It was in the 90s that week but that's not unusual. I was pretty much in the clear. I had gone through several classes without anyone being able to notice. I had covered my scars well. I had covered them so well that I forgot about them by recess.

At recess I went on the playground with everyone else in my class. I played and after about ten minutes I got hot and took off my long sleeve shirt. I thought nothing of it because I had a t-shirt on. But I forgot the lash marks that were on my arms.

Immediately as I exposed my arms one of the kids said" Sig what happened to your arms". I didn't know what to say. I got nervous and stumbled over my words and immediately I thought of the three dogs we had. I then said" Yeah, I was playing rough with our dogs. Joey then said" oh, did it hurt?" I said "Heck yeah it hurt!" I had never felt so relieved, and I thought I was in the clear.

Unbeknownst to me the P.E. teacher had seen me but had not heard my explanation. I saw her talking to my mom in my mom's classroom after school. She had asked what had happened and my mom calmly explained that I had been caught up in a briar patch while visiting our relatives farm. Apparently, I was now Peter Rabbit in Farmer Magnusson's Garden. I wanted to say something, but I knew I could not. So, I stayed quiet and kept it in the family.

This incident made me extremely aware and conscientious of my family. I felt as though I wanted to be unnoticed or else it would draw more attention to my family and my father in particular. I was already a quiet child. I rarely talked in class and almost always followed the rules. I began working on subjects more intently so I could answer questions accurately and not draw any unwanted attention. I don't think teachers ever detected a change. They just saw me as a shy kid.

The next few years in school were "normal". I did well in my classes and continued to interact with classmates such as Thomas. My mother was awarded teacher of the year which of course was good as it helped raise my mother's morale.

My father did little for my mother in the way of showing affection. Never can I recall her receiving flowers, jewelry, or even a card. Birthdays and anniversaries would go by without any celebration. This was true for both my parents. Birthdays of children were seldom celebrated as well. I can recall only two birthday parties I had as a child.

However, I remember attending many parties for friends and relatives. I always felt at parties as though I had been cheated by being in my family. I always felt poor.

While friends were getting all the latest clothes and toys. I was wearing hand me downs that were out of fashion. I occasionally had new clothes, but the majority were not worn only by me.

These feelings only added to my insecurity. Added to that, my name Sigmund is not the most common of American names. I resented the fact I wasn't named something cool like Steve, Jeff, Frank. I had to be Sigmund.

My name was popular with kids, however. It was always funny for the kids when someone called me Sig the pig. Sigmund the Sea Monster, (The Kroft brothers had a popular children's show with that name", or Sig the twig. Even though I tried to avoid attention I got into a few scuffles with other boys because I didn't have to take name calling from them.

On one occasion I got into such a fight that a teacher had to break up the fight between me and another kid. The kid had started to rattle down the list" Siggy the piggy, Sigmund the Sea Monster, Sig the Twig". The kid would just keep on repeating it time after time. I just got so fed up with him taunting and trying to embarrass me in front of friends that I had to do something. Before I knew it, my fist had hit Frank Hull in the nose.

I didn't stop either. I continued to hit this kid. He had been teasing me for months and had been pushing other kids around. He had been asking for it and I decided to give him what he wanted. That was my excuse anyway. I hit him in the face repeatedly and after a minute the teacher, Mrs. Patrick came in and immediately pulled me away from him. I don't even remember if he hit me I just remember that I kicked that little jerk's ass and it felt good.

Of course, I had to go to the principal's office to receive my obligatory paddling, but that was not what I was afraid of, I just knew when I got home my father was going to go berserk with a peach tree switch, belt, bailing wire or some other instrument of punishment and pain. The principle had nothing on my father.

My mom heard the news by the end of the day. She was disappointed, but I know she understood why I reacted the way I did. When my mother told my father about the incident I braced for the worst. My father approached me with his "mad as hell face: and said turn around. I did and he took of his belt and whipped me a few times but it was not as intense as I had felt in the past. He told me "Sigmund I know why you did what you did. I'm glad you stood up for yourself, but you don't have to use violence to get your point across".

Now I was really confused. My father, who had when I was five, beat the shit out of me for hitting my sister and I for lollygagging around before a family trip had just given me a somewhat weak whipping and had told me I was essentially right for standing up for myself. I didn't get it. All the beating, lashings and spankings I had received came from a very mad and enraged man. The last one didn't even rate in comparison to the others. I was not disappointed, just confused because of the inconsistency of it all.

CHAPTER 4

The inconsistency continued with my father for next few years. He would go ballistic at my brother. Other times when it seemed that Emily should be punished for disobeying our mother or father did nothing.

My father had an appreciation for wildlife and animal life in general. He tended to his livestock, chickens, and crops with great care over the next few years. He; however, became remote and sometimes difficult to reach or get his attention.

He was up every morning in his Ford pickup truck and if you watched him after he got done with feeding and watering the cattle with Mr. Thompson you could see my father writing in his journal. If you were to check back on him in a few hours to see if he wanted help he would answer gruffly. "Get out of here" and he would continue writing.

My father's journals soon began to fill up the floorboard of his pickup. My mother took notice of this and approached my father and he said he was keeping records on Aunt Laura for his mom. My mother did not pursue my father with any more questions likely being afraid of where questioning would lead her. She knew her husband would get agitated, and he was become increasingly irritable.

He had become so irritable that I was scared to even approach him. I only dared approach if he wanted me to go to him or needed my help doing something. I did my best to avoid my father. I spent a lot of time playing in the woods near our house, playing with our dogs or the family cat.

Our cat Lucky was a very cool cat to me because whenever I needed him, he was around and unlike most cats he knew when to stay out of the way. This cat was so cool he even played fetch. Every once in a while, he would bring in a dead mouse. He was appreciated for his mouse killing skill.

One spring evening I had spent what seemed like an hour looking for Lucky before I went to bed. I nor my sister, Emily, had any luck finding him. We shook the cat food bag. We called and looked for him with no luck. I went to my bedroom and my mom assured me we would find Lucky. I felt better and fell asleep.

I woke up the next morning and was ready to start looking for Lucky. I had breakfast, at the insistence of my mother. Once I was done eating, I flew out the door. I went back in the back yard, which was an acre. I looked places I could not look the night before due to darkness.

I came upon our garden and I looked around all the plants and up and down all the rows. As I came up to a row of corn, I noticed a brownish furry figure laying on the ground underneath the stalks. I knew this was not Lucky because Lucky had a soft furry grey coat and this animal was dirty. I got closer and I threw up my breakfast all over the ground.

What I'd seen was my favorite cat that had apparently been dragged through the dirt and mud and had been beheaded by a garden hoe. I knew this because the bloody garden hoe was still on the ground and Lucky's head was only inches away from it. I knew my father had done this. I immediately broke into tears and yelled out, "I hate my Daddy". My mother heard this and hurriedly ran out to see what was wrong. When she saw what I had seen she hugged me and tried to console me. But there was no consolation for losing my favorite pet. I now hated my father.

I confronted my father and told him what I had seen, and I asked him why he killed my cat. I told my father that I hated him for what he had done. I braced for the worst, but all I got was a cold distant stare. My father was somewhere else in his head.

Once I got over my loss, I began to try to figure out why my father had killed the cat. I figured maybe he mistook Lucky for a squirrel or rabbit. This, however; was impossible as we had only brown rabbits and brown squirrels on our property. I thought, "What if it was an accident"?

This all was unlikely as my father had better than 20/20 eyesight and had never made a mistake like that before or so it was explained to me. Killing the cat was an intentional act.

I had seen things like my father beheading chickens and hanging them upside down on the clothesline to drain their blood. I had also seen my father shoot a cow in the head after it had broken it's legs. These things were of necessity for food and out of mercy and as a young child growing up on a farm you learned these actions made sense. What didn't make any sense was that Lucky was healthy, served a purpose and my father knew I loved that cat.

My father remained distant, cold, and easily agitated at times. My father's collection of noted pads began to grow and he became increasingly difficult to live with day by day. I avoided him as much as possible. At all times, I would attempt to ask my mother for things. My Dad would either ignore me or smack me across the face for bothering him. He was usually just too irritated to talk. Sometimes he could not be found. To put it mildly, he did not have an open-door policy.

Over the next year my father became ever increasingly agitated. He would often argue with my mother over the least little trivial things and of course my Aunt Laura would creep into the Argument." Why did your mother let Laura have all that money?", my mother would say, or "Did you see Laura in her new Cadillac?"

Laura always found her way into the argument. She was one of those people everybody has in their family but is ashamed to claim. She never held down a job. She had gone through three husbands way before the divorce rate began to skyrocket. In this area, she was ahead of the curve.

One of her husbands died mysteriously of heart attack. It was mysterious because the man had no predisposing factors known to us. None of her children were from the same baby daddy. Yes, each baby had a different daddy. This, however, is common now. Again, she was ahead of the curve. She was also drawing welfare and claiming illness she did not have to qualify for the welfare.

Laura was the poster child for everything that was wrong with the Jimmy Carter era welfare system. She was "that woman" driving up in her Cadillac to pick up her check at the welfare office. If my family had been more prosperous licentious Laura would have never found, her way into the conversation. Though the fact of the matter was that we often scraped by on frozen meat and a teacher's paltry salary of $900 a month for six people in the household. Yes, we were close to the poverty threshold. Laura also caused problems because she was always asking for more! Even after she got her fair share of 25% of the money from the sale of the land she would cry to Zelda for more. It's the old saying, the squeaky wheel always gets the grease. Laura was always squeaking. Zelda always greased her wheel. Aunt Laura would always say that she couldn't afford this or that for the kids.

This was always the cry no matter how true or untrue it was always the same. Had it never occurred to her to GET A JOB!!! My Aunt had used the U.S. government, my family, and who ever she could get her claws into. She was a user with a capitol "U".

She was a waste of human flesh and an irritant to my immediate family as well our cousins. She certainly, didn't cause my father's schizophrenia but she certainly helped to exacerbate it!

The following year after my cat was killed my family was forced to move from the immediate ten acres our home was on. The sale of the land provided my grandmother with money. Guess what member of the family wanted their share first. After all, she coerced my grandmother into forcing my mother and father to sell our land. She just wanted her "fair" share of the land that she had never plowed, tilled, planted or harvested.

We then moved into the suburbs. What a culture shock that was for the family, not least of whom, my father. We went from having a 50-acre backyard to a fenced backyard that was one fifth of an acre. This was a great shock to my cold, distant and easily agitated father.

My father now had a 20-minute drive one way to get to the family ranch/farm. He could no longer get out bed and take a two-minute ride down to the stockyard. This disturbed him and it did so visibly. If you were to watch my father as he left the farm you might notice my father had an aura about him as though he was continually looking over his shoulder. My father continued his note writing and this became more prolific now.

My mother stumbled upon his notes as she had done a few times before. This time there were dozens and dozens of them hidden in his toolbox in his Ford F-150 truck. My father now, after the move, was more worried that someone may be watching. So, he had attempted to hide some of his latest notes. They looked something like: $1/n\{\frac{\frac{2}{88}}{1}\frac{9}{4}\frac{3}{4}\frac{3}{2}$ ßà£¥.H ¥ÉÉ∞. Line after line and page after page of this would be written. No longer was it a mixture of German and English as it had been. It was some sort of unintelligible code.

I'm not sure what, my mother thought and I being as young as I was at eleven didn't know what to think. It was eerie and frightening.

The next week on a cold Thursday in November my mother was bringing Emily home and I from school. As we drove into the driveway, we noticed my father had his axe in his hand. He had not been cutting wood as he always wore his overalls for that. When he saw my mother open her door he commanded my mother, Emily, and I to "Get inside or else", as he brandished his axe in the cold air. He had a cold steely stare and it was obvious he was visibly agitated. We had all seen him like this before and this was usually when all hell broke loose, but never before did he carry a potentially deadly weapon in his hand. My mother said to Michael," There is no way in hell we are going inside with you!"

He then charged at the car with ax in hand my mother immediately put the car into reverse and she pulled out of the driveway as fast as she could. Before we could get too far away my father managed to take a swing at the car with the ax and it hit the windshield.

I saw the axe coming toward me and all I could do was wince and try and get in the back seat. Luckily, the windshield held, and my mother sped down our road in reverse as fast as possible until she was far enough away from my father to turn around.

As we were driving away, we were all in tears. We were scared from what had just happened and we were afraid for Will. We did not know if Will had gotten home from work before my father's episode or not. The first thing we did was to call Will's work to make sure he was there. Will had reported to work at 9 O'clock and was having to work a double. That was probably the only time Will was glad to be working a double shift.

We then went to Amanda's house for a visit. While there, my mother called the police to see if a situation had developed. Unbeknownst to us a few neighbors had seen the entire event. My mother had been aware of this since she had noticed the neighbors as she said were" gawking at us".

My mother told the police that she believed my father was having some sort of psychotic episode. By the time my mother called the police, the police had already apprehended him. Luckily for Michael when he saw the police uniforms it triggered something in his mind and he supposedly threw his axe down. He had been brandishing it in our front yard, as neighbors looked on, for over thirty minutes after we had fled from him.

He managed to threaten all the neighbors if they came near. I'm sure he scared quite a few as they all waited for the police before doing anything.

I'm certain that if my father had not thrown down the axe after police started to approach him, then more than likely he would have been shot dead. In the early 1980s police had much more leeway with use of deadly force than in today's politically correct environment. He was fortunate to have only a few bumps and bruises from the scuffle the police had to make to get him down. He could be one ornery son of a bitch.

27

My mother was a wreck by the end of the day. Her husband had just tried to assault her and two of her children with an axe. He then harassed neighbors and was arrested by the police. Us and Will were going to be spending the next few days at Amanda and Robert's.

My mother had a mess of insurance papers, court papers, and psychiatric facilities to look at.

We were visited by our parish priest and other well-wishers while at Amanda's. Of course, once we returned home my mother had to deal with neighbors to squelch the rumor mill. My mother had told them all what was going on with my father and they were genuinely sympathetic, but none were particularly helpful. They just wanted to know dirt about what was going on.

After a few months while my father was away in a psychiatric facility receiving "therapy" things began to settle down at the Magnusson household. Emily was doing well in school again. I was playing organized baseball and doing well. Will got promoted at work. However, things were never going to be the same again. They had never been great but things at the Magnussen household had never been this unsettled. What had happened to our Daddy?

CHAPTER 5

Growing Pains

The year following my father's initial hospitalization for psychiatric help; I adjusted well in his absence. I played football in the fall and did well. I gained confidence in myself and what I was capable of doing when given good direction. I felt no loss from my father's absence at my games. If anything, I felt relief.

From time-to-time kids and parents would ask where my father was. My standard line if asked, was that he just couldn't make it. I would never elaborate why my father couldn't make it. Occasionally, people might press me or my mother for an answer and we would let them know he was in the hospital.

We never let them know for what reason or why he was hospitalized. It wasn't their business anyhow, and usually once people knew he was in the hospital the questions would stop. But the occasional pestering person would pester on and the response was "Why do you need to know?" I was always petrified that someone might actually find out what was wrong with my father. I could just imagine what people would say if they found out." No wonder Sig behaves the way he does. His father's a whacko. "Because of this fear, I always tried to walk the straight and narrow path. I avoided fights did my homework and studied to avoid being reprimanded and drawing unnecessary attention.

After all, my mother was a teacher at my school and if I did something wrong, I knew my mother would hear about it quickly. My school had already demonstrated that to me.

The year had passed with my father being in treatment on and off throughout the school year. I remember my father's first visit home being somewhat awkward. I was scared, ashamed, and anxious. I just knew my father would sense how I felt and thought surely, he would beat me. However, this was a Haldol medicated Michael Magnusson that was much calmer and colder than before. It was strange how he hugged me with glazed eyes went to the Lazy Boy rocking chair.

My father was quite a different man when he was taking his medication. He was much calmer and not nearly as agitated as he had been. I could actually talk to him and ask him to play catch without him blowing up or hitting me. I think my father's Haldol did as much for me as it did for my father.

Haldol, of course is no walk in the park. It is a powerful antipsychotic drug that can cause extreme somnolence and catatonia. This did not happen to my father. I never witnessed him in a catatonic state from Haldol nor somnolence. He was simply sluggish and a little slower than usual.

In the early 1980s there were not a whole lot of other anti-psychotic meds that were available to my father's psychiatrists: Haldol, Stelazine, and Cogentin were the meds of choice. As is typical with most patients and psychiatric patients as was with my father he was not 100% compliant as he preferred to "think clearly" in place of the sluggishness he experienced from Haldol.

My father's non-compliance with taking his psych. meds caused quite a number of unpleasant situations to occur that otherwise might have been avoided had he been following his medication protocol. This fact made me constantly leery of being with my father in public because I just never knew when he might "lose it". Being a boy in puberty I was already self-conscious and to throw in a father recently diagnosed as a paranoid homicidal schizophrenic and you too might have some real issues regarding self-confidence.

When I played baseball that summer, I wondered if my mother was going to bring my father to the games. My brother Will, would go to some of the games. My sister, Emily would go from time to time with my mom and only once ever did my father go. All but one of the ten games I pitched, my father was content to stay in his Lazy Boy chair and at the time it was fine with me. I was extremely conscientious of myself. Luckily, I was a good enough pitcher that I drew praise from my teammates and coaches. This helped me a great deal.

On the one occasion my father did go. I was so nervous about the game I forgot about him and he did behave himself. I can only imagine what it would have been like, if my father had not been medicated and had one of his hallucinogenic episodes. He might have begun to take off all his clothes in public and run around calling people all sorts of ethnic slurs as he had been reported doing while hospitalized. He might have run onto the field and hit me as he had done before while we were playing catch. He could be utterly unpredictable and potentially endlessly embarrassing. Who knows though? An incident like that in public might have been liberating as it would have unmasked what our family and other families like ours were "hiding" due to similar problems. However, more than likely it would have brought us shame, embarrassment and potentially ridicule as even today at the initial writing of this in 2002 mental illness is misunderstood and is treated with social stigma. In the current time of 2022 things are not much better.

I will never know the alternative to the events of that year and summer. I only know what happened to me and how I felt at the time. I later found out how my brother Will felt.

That summer Will had just received a promotion at his job. Apparently, he was an exemplary employee with a good work ethic. He also got his opportunity in this new position to hook up with fellow co-workers and he was introduced to Mary Jane. He found her to be quite relaxing. She lifted the weight of Will's stress, from his upbringing, from his recent rejection by girls, off his shoulders.

Mary Jane was cheap, affordable, and easily accessible.

I remember on several occasions hanging out with Will and his new friends and helping them roll their joints. I was all of 12 years old. I don't think I even realized it was illegal. To their credit they never offered me a joint to smoke but I was around it and unlike Slick Willy I did inhale. I had to breathe after all. They were probably just happy to have someone along who would take the work out of fun or simply share the fun with.

I followed Will as much as possible. I was desperate for a role model and Will was the only one available on a regular basis and he was pretty cool with me. After all, he never beat me or told me to get the hell away.

I think I learned as many lessons on what not to do as what you should do from Will. He wound up in jail a couple of times for DUI over the next couple of years. My mother, of course, was very upset with this as she was raised in a household where drinking alcohol was not tolerated. She wanted to raise her children with the same philosophy that the only alcohol in the house comes from baking bread made with yeast.

can only imagine what my mother thought when Will began experimenting with cocaine. By the time we realized Will was using cocaine it was almost too late.

Will gradually became reclusive from the family and spent less and less time with his little brother. The time I did spend with him he was usually going to the local pawn shops to pawn something for money.

The first item missing from our house was his stereo, then the T.V., VCR, shotguns, etc. Will nearly ran himself out of his new townhouse and home. He nearly lost his townhome. Our mom was first to notice that Will was having a problem. Getting him to admit it and go into therapy was a difficult task as it always is for addicts. It is always ultimately their choice and their choice alone.

CHAPTER 6

Rock Bottom

As you already know I helped Will and his friends roll joints and like good old' Slick Willie I never smoked them either, but I sure was around them and couldn't help but inhale. I just never put one up to my lips. So, I technically never did anything illegal myself regarding intentional intake of a controlled substance. However, I would have been found guilty by association. If I had ever been caught helping my brother and his friends, they likely would have been charged with corruption of a minor. We all could have been in real trouble. Luckily, this never happened. It is rather amazing though that two times Will had been arrested for DUI and he had marijuana in his possession. Fortunately, for Will or maybe unfortunately for Will the Kansas state Highway Patrol on both occasions did not search his vehicle. If they had searched Will's truck, he would have spent more than a night in jail and would have had a serious court date. In the 1980's the state of Kansas wasn't particularly hard on DUIs. He was lucky in that respect also. These close brushes with the law that Will had didn't seem to have much of an effect. I can remember the day Will got out from jail. He rushed to a certain parcel of land on the farm.

Will had planted in a secluded area and in it was a patch of marijuana plants so he could water them. I guess he was afraid the hot Kansas sun was going to scorch his precious crop.

When I went out with him, I couldn't believe my eyes. He had a crop of marijuana plants the size of a Large 50 by 50-foot garden. Cheech and Chong would have been proud.

Being the dutiful young brother that I was I helped Will transport 10 gallons of water by 5-gallon buckets about 500 yards. I did this with Will on several occasions week as a 12-year-old. It's no wonder all the sports coaches were impressed with how much muscle I was putting on. If they only knew how I was putting it on!? Who says marijuana can't be beneficial.

Will, eventually graduated from his indoctrination with marijuana and began using Cocaine and crack. This graduation created a whole new set of dynamics for Will. I can't say exactly how Will was introduced to cocaine or how long he used cocaine.

Once Will began using cocaine, he had much less contact with me and the rest of the family. I was in high school at this time. I was making a transition to a new peer group and being a typical teenager, I spent less time watching Will. I had more concern with my own status among my peers. I don't know if this had any effect on Will, but I knew he started hanging around a different group of people and more specifically different women. I have no doubt the potential for sex with these women had a great impact on Will's desire to use cocaine.

These women were cocaine users, and no doubt saw Will as their ticket to a fresh powder trail. Will, like most men were more than likely eager to do whatever he could to gain sexual favors with these women. Will did not have the best of luck with women and did not have good relationships with girls when he was in high school. No doubt, Will's lack of confidence with women was likely due to the fact we lacked a sound father figure and our mother had too much on her plate.

t's somewhat easy to see how Will was seduced. A young man on his own, making decent money, and has not had the best of luck with women is going to be easy prey for a young woman in search of a good time if that young man is willing to pay the way.

To make a reference to Metallica, Will became mastered by his addiction. He chopped his breakfast on a mirror and soon his life had no rhyme or reason. Will lost so much of what he earned with his hard-earned pay checks because of his habit. But this wasn't enough in itself to hit rock bottom.

Every addict has a different road to reaching rock bottom. Some can afford their habit so those few suffer no immediate financial consequences. So, they continue their habit until they lose a spouse, a loved one, get caught committing a crime or die. For the addicts that aren't as financially set all of the same things happen except the financial toll hits much earlier. Some people hit the addiction so fast that they go straight through rock bottom to six feet under. This happened to one of Will's coke buds. Luckily, it didn't happen to Will; although, he did come close.

When I was about 14, one early morning, our household received a call from the emergency room at the local hospital. The call came at about 3:30 a.m. My mom woke up to answer the phone. I woke up just after my mom did. I asked my mom what had happened. She waved me off as she always did and still does when she's concentrating on something. I knew from past experiences and other people's wisdom that nothing good ever happens after 2:00 in the morning.

The thoughts raced through my head as to what could be happening. My immediate thought was that my father had done something, or something had been done to him at his latest institution of psychiatry.

I imagined that my father had possibly gone berserk and had attacked and seriously injured his doctor, nurse, or one of his mental health aids. My father had attempted to attack one of his psychiatrists at another hospital. As I was told, Michael got as far as jumping over the psychiatrist's desk and putting the good doctor in a stranglehold. Luckily, for the psychiatrist he had some sort of martial arts training and was able to free himself and subdue my father. So, as you can imagine, my father was a strong candidate for the cause of the early morning phone call.

I then thought that something might have happened to Emily. You hear so often of how college students are killed or maimed in car wrecks overnight due to drunken driving, either through their own indiscretion or someone else's. That though was quickly dashed because it was early Friday morning and Emily was not so likely to be out partying and even less likely with classes the next morning.

Amanda was also a poor candidate for the early morning phone call. She was married with a six- year old daughter and had a good job to go to the next morning. It was just unlikely she was the reason for the call.

Will was the only one left and Will was the cause of the phone call. Will had been taken to the emergency room by ambulance with a stab wound to his rib cage. Will had gotten into an altercation with another man because of a woman

Apparently, Will had been seeing a married woman. This woman was a cocaine addict like Will. She had been using Will as a ticket for free powder or at least more of it. According to Will, she said she was going leave her husband, but I don't think her husband had the same plans for her.

When this man found Will with his wife, he did what a lot of men would probably do if they found their wife with another man. This man went for the first weapon he could find, and he stabbed Will with a kitchen knife under Will's left arm.

The married woman Will was seeing had apparently called the ambulance. However, she was nowhere around the emergency room when my mother and I got there. The only thing we saw will lay in the hospital bed with chest tubes to prevent his left lung from collapsing.

My mother and I had arrived at the emergency room at about 5:00 am and waited until 7:00 am to see him. Will had needed a thoracotomy for chest tube placement and he wasn't placed in a regular hospital room until 7:00am or so. Will woke up later that morning. When he did, he woke up in more than one way.

About a week later Will was in drug counseling classes and was in a

36

group home temporarily for about a four to six-week period. During this period of time, Will had the unique opportunity to examine his life and figure out how in the hell he got where he was.

I went with my mother to a few of Will's 12-step program classes. These were family meetings in which all of the addict's families could get together and discuss social and family issues. I didn't see any other of the facets of the program Will was in, I did find the family meetings to be informative and helpful. I was hopeful Will felt the same way.

When Will got out of the group home he continued to attend weekly meetings and began going to church on a regular basis. Will's Life began to turn around and improve from this point on.

Will has not had a perfect life since, but he has been able to have a functional life. Will is currently remarried with a child from his previous marriage. He recently received another promotion from the company which he has worked for many years. They stayed with him throughout his ordeal with drugs and gave him a second chance. That second chance was not always available from other companies. Will was fortunate in that aspect. Not all companies in corporate America are apathetic to employee moraleand needs and today its seems that is continuing to improve.

Aside from the occasional call from his ex-wife asking for more money than mandatory child support requires, Will's been living a relatively good life and that surely beats pushing up daisies from six feet under. That is a vast improvement over hitting rock bottom.

CHAPTER 7

Standing Up

After seeing what Will went through as a drug addict and then watching him go through counseling and recovery, I had a fairly good idea at fourteen that drugs weren't a good idea. I had a good peer group to hang around with and we pretty much knew who all the "druggies" were, and we avoided them and made fun of them as though they were the village idiots.

Of course, I wasn't about to let any one of my friends know what Will had been doing and what I had done previously to help him grow his marijuana crop. I was a hypocrite. I had an image to maintain and a peer group to hang around. I wasn't going to let anyone know any of my secrets. How many teenagers would accept into their circle of friends a kid with a schizophrenic father who was in and out of mental health institutions and who also had brother who was a drug addict?

I took great stock in the adage Benjamin Franklin once used, "The best kept secret is the one you keep to yourself." I'm pretty sure my mom did as well. I seriously doubt she would have been keen to share our family situation with her fellow teachers. I certainly wasn't going to spout out our situation to my friends who all lived in well to do neighborhoods and had apparently "healthy" family situations. That would have been teenage class suicide. You all know how cruel teenagers can be. No thank you!

I did my best to maintain my status at school. I studied at home. I consistently practiced my trumpet and I practiced pitching in my yard throwing a baseball at a wooden target I had made. I lifted weights with a religious fervor. At the end of the school year, I thought to myself," Thank God I made it through another school year without anybody finding out the secrets of my life". I did this every year at the end of the school year and by the grace of God I managed to keep my family secret in the closet.

That summer, when I turned 15, my father was released from yet another stay at a mental health facility. It was not the best summer, but it could have been worse. It is never a good idea to combine a15-year-old with surging testosterone and a paranoid homicidal schizophrenic man. It's a potentially combustible situation that can't be easily extinguished.

My father had so dominated me in the years before. I knew I was going to make damn sure he didn't dominate me and make me feel less than human again. Why did any father have to behave that way?

From the time I was a small child whenever I said something oppositional to my father, even the least trivial thing, it always came to blows whether by fist or with a two by four. I was always on the receiving end and it did not help that I was taught a child is never to hit your parent.

I could have a discussion with him at the breakfast table over the score of the Kansas City Royal's game and he would go psychotic on me out of nowhere. He would get up out of his seat and bull rush me to knock me down and proceed to hit me in the face, abdomen, or any place he wanted. It didn't really matter what we could be talking about. When he got a certain look in his eyes, I knew what was about to happen. It could be a discussion about having a soda, getting a haircut, going out with friends or the score of a baseball game I was going to end up taking it and it happened over and over and time andtime again.

One time in particular my father had been keeping Pepsi locked in his truck's toolbox because he did not want to share it with anyone. I asked him if I could have some and he said no. I then came back to him a few minutes later with fifty cents (vending machine price at the time) and asked him if I could have some and he said no. Oh boy was that a mistake. Before I could say" Oh no!" My old man was leaping out of his lazy boy recliner and was charging at me. I then found myself up against the wall and he continued to use me as a tackling dummy for at least a couple of minutes. He then said," Leave me alone you little bastard.

When I say no, that means no!" Of course, after this I was a wreck. I lay huddled on the floor crying. All I could think of was how it wasn't right.

I went back to my room and just laid down on my bed thinking of why my life had to be this way.

Another time, it was during the school year and I needed to get a haircut. My Mom was ready to go to the store and I was supposed to go with her to get my hair cut. It was about 1:00 pm on a Saturday and I was watching a sports show with Will. My mom implored me to leave but the show wasn't done, and I made the mistake of saying no. I don't want to leave yet. With that response my father rose up from his Lazy Boy recliner and proceeded to give me a good old fashion belt whoopin'. It must have taken me a Few seconds for me to get to my feet and when I did finally get up, I got a nice flurry of punches to the mid-section and face. When my father decided he needed a breather. My mother said," Come on Sig, let's go". Marie never attempted to stop Michael. I think she knew better. Though looking back on it, she was complicit in the behavior.

Then there was another incident when I was about 10 years old. I decided I wanted to play a game with my brother Will that I had learned at school. This game frogger was a game where kids at school had been trading hits on the shoulder until one of the kids would cry mercy. Will didn't have a problem playing. He was likely high at the time anyway. I traded a couple of hits with Will and then Will hit back and I made short, small "ow!" and Michael heard it. He ran towards us like a flash into the bedroom and started beating me. He hit me in the face and mid-section for what seemed like a solid minute. He threw me onto the bed and hit me a few more times in the face for good measure. I missed school for remainder of the week because there was no way my mom could explain away the black and blue face I had. I looked like I'd been a boxing match and had gone at least five rounds. I was treated like I was sickor something.

This was true in a twisted sort of way. The bad thing was that my father was at home all week long. It was wintertime and there wasn't a whole lot of farming going on. He might leave for an hour or so to go feed the cattle. He would come then come back home and we'd have the rest of the day the spend together and that's how the rest of the week played out. I did a whole lot of reading.

I read Tolkien, Dostoyevsky, Orwell, and other authors whose works were written years ahead of my reading ability at that age. However, I would do anything to overcome the boredom and minimize any interaction I might have with my father.

I would stay in the bedroom all day long and read until my mother would get home from teaching school. I avoided lunch time to avoid my father. I would do just about anything that week to avoid him. I would rather go hungry than have an encounter with my father.

I had just known that when I turned 15 and I saw my father again, things were going to be different. I had stopped hauling water buckets for my brother so I started lifting weights. I managed to put on a good amount of muscle over the year and by that summer I was five feet eight inches tall and 160 lbs. I wasn't going to be dominated anymore.

To my surprise my father seemed to be pretty docile. He stayed on his regimen of anti-psychotic meds and we got along pretty well. We even had some lively arguments without any bull rushing. Wow, now that's progress.

But don't think I wasn't waiting for it. I actually had some fun with the old man. We played catch a few times. Will, Dad and I even dug a few fence postholes and we literally mended some fences. We did a lotof farm work. Except for two occasions that will be forever etched in my mind, it wasn't as bad a summer as it nearly turned out to be.

41

The first occasion occurred just after the July 4th Holiday. My Dad had been off his Haldol for about a week. I guess he had been pocketing the medication in his cheeks as he drank his water. My Mom could be duped somewhat easily. Manipulative Michael did it again.

The afternoon on the 5th of July that year my father went berserk. He started hallucinating that he was on the farm and people were trying to rustle our cattle. I just happened to be in my room when I heard him yelling." You sorry fuckers get off my land." I was just stupid enough to come out of my room to see what was happening. I didn't have the foresight to think" Sig, ya think your old man is having another paranoid hallucination"? That's exactly what was happening. As soon as I entered into the living room my father entered into his bull rushing stance and made his way straight for me. I knew in a split second I had to act and as fast as my nervous system could send the impulse from my brain to my shoulder, I was rearing back my fist and I had clocked my old man right in the jaw. I saw him stop and stagger and then I made my bull rush and got him on the ground, my mother, who had been taking refuge in the kitchen with phone in hand, acted as fast to get my dad's medication and put in his mouth with tongs. She then checked his mouth with them to make sure he had swallowed. She surely didn't want to lose a finger. Having a finger bitten off by your husband doesn't look good.

The whole time when I was holding my father down, he was cursing." You sorry thieving niggers. I'm going to fix you." His voice was tired, dejected, and pathetic. At a time when I should have been feeling a sense of pride for standing up to my abusive father; I felt a very awkward sense of pity and guilt. I felt pity for the sad defeated man that lay before me and guilt for hitting my parent. You know the good book says a child should never strike their parent. Yet, I did. I had to. What else was I to do? What if he had gotten to one of his rifles?

I spent a long time justifying my actions to myself. My mother said I had done what I had to do. Will agreed with our mom. Amanda and Emily were both oblivious to what had happened, as they were soengrossed in their own lives. When they found out what had happened, they both had the same sort of "Why did Sig do that?" response. My sisters could be so clueless sometimes.

The next day my father woke up with a nice lump on his jaw and cheek. What a change; instead of receiving it I dished it out! I felt good, but in a guilty sort of way. I was just happy things hadn't gotten too messy. But I knew If I had to defend myself I could do it again. That was empowering.

Well wouldn't you know I got another chance later in the summer. It was mid-August and my mother had decided to go for elective surgery to have her gallbladder removed. It had been causing her intense abdominal pain. My mom had made arrangements for my dad and I. Will was supposed to check on usafter work.

By this time, Will was a recovering addict. I was to stay with my friend Thomas for a couple of days. I would have preferred to stay with them longer, but they had planned an end of summer vacation and were to be heading to the Caribbean on my mom's third day in the hospital. So, by the middle of the week I was back at the Magnusson homestead.

Will had been checking in on our father and he told me how he was holding up over the phone while I was at Thomas' family's house. It seemed like old man Magnusson had been taking his meds and had even managed to do some farm work. That was a relief. I felt pretty sure I would be okay when I went back home.

My first day back home everything went pretty well. I got back in the afternoon and my father greeted me with his typical "Hello, Sig." I reciprocated. Everything seemed okay. We made dinner that night and watched the Kansas City Royals game on the T.V.

The next morning, I woke up and went for a run around the neighborhood. It was a cool morning in Kansas terms. It was about 76°F. When I got back my father had already had breakfast, so I made my own. So far so good I thought. That afternoon, we went to the local mechanics for a new battery for our International Harvester. We then went out to the farm to put it in to make sure it worked. While my father was putting in the battery I was spreading out bales of hay for our cattle and set out cattle cubes in the feed trough for them.

Once we got done it was about 98°F around 5:00 pm. We went home and we sat in front of the T.V. watching the evening news. Later we ate dinner around 6:30 pm and then watched the Kansas City Royals game. Thank God for baseball.

Will came by and guess what was for dinner? That's right, beef! That's one thing we could almost always count on. The night was pretty uneventful. That was until 2:00 am when my father woke up with another episode of a hallucination. I would have been content to weather out another storm, but I heard a lot of dishes being broken, and I heard our Irish Setter yelp outside. Hearing our dog yelp outside torqued me off and I wasn't going to let the same thing that happened to my cat Sparky happen to our Irish Setter Kris. I came out of my bedroom to see what my crazy ass dad might be doing again. When I got to the end of the hallway my father greeted me with a 30/30 marlin rifle in my face. I just about pissed in my pants. I just new at the ripe old age of 15 my psychotic father was going to blow my head off and I hadn't even gotten laid yet. I was going to be killed because he was hallucinating that I was some thief that had broken into the house and was trying to rob him. I tried to do my best to stay calm.

I said in as calm a voice as I could muster with a 30-caliber weapon in my face," Dad, it's your son Sigmund". Then he said," No you're not! You're just a thieving nigger"! I then said" If I were a thief, how would I know that mom is in the hospital and the cut you have on your arm is from this afternoon when your hand slipped putting the battery in the tractor"? At that point my father started to lower his rifle. I immediately began to slowly push it away and I guess the jerk of my push combined with my father's finger pressure on the trigger made the rifle discharge. The sound of the round discharging from the firearm snapped my father out of his hallucination and scarred the shit out of me and put a new additional peephole in our front door. Luckily, our whole neighborhood was still asleep.

Immediately, my father went to take his medication on the kitchen counter. He suddenly realized what he had almost done. But I don't think he truly realized what he'd nearly done until he'd been medicated for a few days. I didn't call the police because I didn't want to draw any attention, but at the same time I wanted to call them because my father had just about killed me.

Needless to say, I spent a couple of days over at Will's. We came in to check on the old man but there was no way in hell I was going to stick around for more than a few minutes after what had nearly happened. That would be like swimming back to see the shark that nearly took off your leg. No thanks!!

After my mom got back from the hospital, my father seemed his usual self. He took his meds regularly. Marie read Michael the riot act and said in effect if anything like that happened again, he would find himself in jail. The message stuck with him for a while.

CHAPTER 8

Stelazine Dream

My father managed to restrain himself from many altercations with me over the next few months, which was the beginning of the school year. Things were pretty calm at home, relatively speaking. I began the school year and met up with the same old clique I had hung around the previous year. Nothing had changed. Yet it had. I had changed. I had more confidence in myself. Instead of simply doing my schoolwork, I interacted with the teacher in class lectures. Instead of waiting for the teacher to get to me with a question I got to them first and would often answer their question for them. I did this regardless of what class it was; English, Geometry, History, German it didn't matter.

I had been good in classes before. I had managed straight A's before, but this year was going to be an exceptional year. I already had respect from all the jocks, now I was getting respect from the other students. I was becoming more than the shy and introverted "I don't want to draw attention to me" Sigmund Magnusson.

I quit football that year mainly because of the position I played and the lack of playing time I received. I also wanted to take my place in the marching band because the truth of the matter was, I was a better trumpet player than an offensive lineman. This decision paid as my school band won all of our marching competitions and made it all the way to Kansas state finals and we won that too. At that time, being part of that was one of the greatest experiences of my life. I was part of a championship organization. How many teenagers could say that?

I also started my first job that year working at a local store as a clerk. I was excelling in classes, my band won the state championship, and I was making a regular paycheck at my first summer job. The year was turning out to be fairly good.

Then one night in December my father decided he needed to walk to the local grocery store. This is no big deal, but my father in all his paranoid state of mind decided he needed to take his rifle with him. I didn't even know he left the house. My mother sure did notice that he had left but she didn't realize he had the rifle. Apparently, as soon as my dad left my mother came running to the back of the house where Will and I were. She said," You have to go get him before he does something stupid!" she said in a shrill voice. So, Will and I took off after him. When we got to him, he was about two miles away from the house. By the time we got to him the police had my father prostrate on the ground. Will and I figured either the police just happened to be right there, which hardly ever happens in my experience, or somebody had spotted him and tipped off the police. Either way, my father was on the ground with an officer's knee in his back because in all likelihood he had resisted or provoked the officer's in some way.

Thanks be to God, nothing serious happened to anyone. However, I did have a remarkably close call for me with some friends. You see, as the police cruiser pulled away there stood my brother and I at the intersection. At that moment, a car pulled up to the stoplight. A loud voice cried out "Hey Sig, what are you doing with the cops?" I didn't immediately recognize the car or the voices but then I saw the faces I thought what the hell am I going to tell them?" It was a couple of girls who I knew from band. Then it came to me. I said, "We were given a ticket for jaywalking". They actually bought it. I felt so relieved. I took a bunch of ragging at school the next week for jaywalking, but that was nothing compared to the awkwardness that it could have been.

My father was then once again bound for yet another stay at another fine mental health facility. I was both relieved and distressed at this. I would be yet again explaining where my father was, but I didn't have to worry about being bull rushed either. Yin and Yang what can you say?

My father remained in that particular mental health facility for the next three months. This time when he came back home there was little fight left in my father's eyes. He had a Stelazine glaze over his eyes. He was calm but it seemed as if he was not there. It was both sad and relieving.

I continued to do my thing doing my homework, music practice, weightlifting and he sat in his recliner. I remained glad when I left the house whenever I could. I just wanted to get away. The less I stayed at home the better I felt.

I continued to stay busy to avoid my father and my mother who was becoming neurotic likely due to the stress of having to deal with my father day in and day out. Even though I stayed busy and avoided my home situation as much as possible I could never completely get away from it. It was like a cancerous tumor that you could excise but it just kept growing back

Michael had to do it again. One day, after I got home from work, I was outside one of my friend's houses shooting the breeze with him when all of a sudden, I see an ambulance headed down the road to my house. I thought, what the hell could it be now? We raced toward my house and the ambulance was already leaving. My friend and I got in his car and followed the ambulance to the hospital. When we got to the hospital, we met my mom and Will there. My mom thanked David for giving me a ride to the hospital and politely dismissed him from the situation, he obliged.

After our neighbor David left, I found out what had happened. Yet again, Michael had managed to avoid taking his Stelazine. Then after about three days off his medication my father started having vivid hallucinations again. According to Will, who had been taking a nap, my father had stripped down to his underwear and was throwing things as well as my mother around the house.

My brother's sleep was broken by my mother's screams. When Will got up our father was running around the house like a wild man half naked in his underwear and our mother was screaming for help. Will came out and tried to ask our father to stop, but of course, Michael heard none of it. He called them filthy niggers and then tried to attack Will. My brother Will, used the strategy that worked for me and gave our father a pop in the jaw and wrestled him to the ground and kept him there until the ambulance came.

My father had had yet another paranoid delusion, He managed to break two of my mother's ribs and got his own jaw broken, all in a day's work for Michael, my father. He was once again bound for another stay at a psychiatric facility.

Will and I were left to take care of our cattle herd of about 50 cattle. It was pretty routine, rounding up the cattle in that old 1960s model pick up with the column gear shift. I would put the pickup in first and never needed to go beyond second gear to catch up and head off cattle while honking the horn to get them running toward the cattle pen where they would get hay or cattle cubes and hundreds of gallons of water.

We had several cows that had been bred that previous Spring and we had several live births of healthy Hereford cross calves. There was however, one cow that was a little bigger than the others and we fully expected her to have twins. One late February afternoon we were waiting for her to give birth but it did not happen the way we expected. She appeared to not be in any distress, however, the next evening when we went to take care of the herd, we could not find her. We knew that cattle will sometimes go to give birth in a somewhat hidden location if they have the opportunity.

Will got the flashlight from the truck. We looked from one tree line to another across a couple of hundred acres and could not locate her. At about an hour after dark, we stopped our search as Will thought it might

49

be pointless as most likely she was somewhere safe and keeping quiet with her new calf or calves.

We came back the next evening around dusk to take care of the cattle. We did not see our missing cow or see any extra calves. We proceeded to feed the cattle as usual. After taking care of the cattle Will and I took off toward a tree line adjacent to the feedlot. We walked about 200 feet and then we came across an unpleasant smell. Then we saw what we did not want to see but is sometimes a reality in farming.

That poor cow did have twin calves that apparently got tangled in each other and the calf nearest the birth canal had become breech. It would have been an impossible situation for Will and I. Neither Will and certainly, I did not have any ability to reorient a breech calf and save the mother and calves even if we had been there. It was unfortunate. I felt bad about it even though nothing could have been done.

That following weekend we brought diesel, hay, and wood to burn the cow and unborn calves on a cold early March late afternoon and evening. There Will and I sat listening to Led Zeppelin on the radio and watching as the cow and calves were given a hasty cremation. As I sat watching the cow burn, I could only think of what a waste it was. It was just so frustrating like much of my childhood. There was just so much that I could not do or help.

CHAPTER 9

Crossroads

The upcoming year brought up a host of choices that any teenager has to deal with. I had taken my SATs and found I was college bound, so to speak, so I began submitting applications for scholarships and colleges. I looked at a few of the colleges in Kansas. However, for whatever reason, I did not pursue my search or application process as most parent driven teenagers do. I did not start as early as I should have and started my application late in the fall to early winter. As a result, many of the scholarships I was competing for I was at a disadvantage for due to my late applications. With my home situation as it existed, healthcare costs, my families recent funding of my sister's education at an expensive private college, my father's recent hospitalizations my family I knew was strapped for cash. The only way I was going to college now was to earn a scholarship for music or academics at a smaller school. I was facing mounting pressure over what I was going to do with my life.

However, I remembered the visit paid to our high school band by Marine Corps Recruiters. They were very impressive to this young man. They were well spoken, sharp in appearance and message. Of course, every year at a certain Kansas band competition the Unites States Marine Corps Drum and & Bugle Corps performed, and they were impressive in sound and appearance. Every year, they managed to make an impression.

They presented me with an option I really hadn't thought about, and I really did not consider until I heard the message of the recruiters a second time from mouths of my fellow students. The message is well known to many parents, who may look at it as a risky proposition, but to teenagers such as myself it offered me a route of escape far away from my abusive home environment with the prospect of earning money to save for college while in the U.S. Marines. I could additionally take advantage of the Montgomery G.I. bill after receiving an Honorable Discharge after four years of service on active duty. This was just the opportunity I needed but had not thought of prior to that November. The more I thought about it the more I thought of the great benefits.

The more I thought about the potential positive outcomes of what I could have the more I liked the possibility. I would be able to do something I loved to do and be paid for it. I would also get the opportunity to travel and see the U.S. and who knows where else I could be stationed.

I found out from a friend how to contact the Recruiter that came to visit the band. The Recruiter seemed eager to meet with me especially when he found out I was interested in joining the band field.

I met with the Recruiter one night in early November. I was shown different military occupational specialties (M.O.S.s) and was given a very impressive list of famous U.S. Marines. A few names on the list were John Glenn, Lee Marvin, Ted Williams, and many more familiar names. Then I was given a quick battery of tests on arithmetic and vocabulary consisting of about 100 questions a piece with a time limit of 60 seconds to perform. I did well on both. The goal was to see how many questions you could answer correctly and with accuracy. It was a simple test to see how I performed under pressure.

The Recruiter was excited and urged me to contact him later. I remember leaving the Recruiter's office thinking I was important and had potential to be someone. This was a feeling strangely enough that I did not encounter in school or even from my mother; at least that I could remember, I Sig Magnusson, had great potential and was being told I could be somebody.

What a different and attractive message I had received from the Recruiter. It was just so contrary to what I was receiving at home. I knew I was better than my homelife, but when homelife is as odd as I perceived my childhood to be than you can imagine I felt that I had I experienced a warped reality regarding familial relationships as opposed to how I felt familial relationships should be. I had always felt I had something to hide rather than be proud of. I had always had a part of me that said, I am Sig Magnusson, the son of a violent abusive, homicidal paranoid schizophrenic father, could I be more than just an apple not far fallen from the apple tree.

I felt I could be. I wasn't going to be fatalistic. I wanted to be like Huck Finn and escape from my father's sickness and start a new and better life for me. So, I took a chance and signed papers that committed me to enlist in the Marine Corps.

The chance I was taking was that I was generally enlisting in the Marine Corps and I did not have an official audition, which if I made the band would guarantee me a spot for military school, after boot camp, from which I would graduate and join up with a field band or, so I was told.

That December I had my M.E.P.S. date. I arrived there on a Friday evening and took the ASVAB battery of tests. The next morning, I was up with the rest of the recruits (about 200 of us) for the physical. I passed both with flying colors. I didn't realize how well I passed the ASVAB testing until later in boot camp.

The following Spring, I had my audition for the Marine Band Program. I was the last of five to audition. I played a couple of prepared pieces, meaning I had practiced them ad nauseum. I was asked to play about six different pieces of various degrees of difficulty. I performed each piece for the Marine Officer with minimal mistakes while sight reading each of them. Sight reading means seeing it for the first time with no prior practice. For a young musician, sight reading is one of the most difficult tasks to master. It is essentially seeing a piece for the first time and being able to perform it to the best of your ability. At my audition I played it well enough for the Marine Officer to tell me I had a spot. He seemed very pleased.

My making a spot in the Marine Band was one of the most exciting things I had ever accomplished in my life. It was exhilarating and I was on a high for the remainder of the school year knowing I would be escaping my home environment and on the way to an adventure in the military. Some of my friends couldn't believe what I was doing or why. If they only knew.

My next step was to take an oath to defend America from all threats either foreign or domestic as well as other things and I was on my way to being part of one of the most heralded military services in the United States and possibly even in the world. Oddly enough a film made by Stanley Kubrick called "Full Metal Jacket" had influenced my decision about the Marine Corps. I figured that if I ever had to go in to battle for the service of my country I might as well be trained by the best Warriors the U.S. military had to offer.

After another final day at the M.E.P.S station I was set to report to boot camp that July 18. My future awaited me. I was willing, able, and ready to go. I just had to wait.

CHAPTER 10

USMC

Once I graduated from high school, I just tried to prepare myself for the physical rigors I was expecting in Marine Corps boot camp. My workouts included running three miles every other day, doing pull ups and sit ups three to four times a week. What concerned me though was the same as what concerned so many other recruits for the Marine Corps. I had been warned about the psychological tricks the Drill Instructors would play on the recruits; however, compared to some of the psychological problems I had to deal with at home I figured any psych job I got in bootcamp couldn't be any worse than what I had experienced at home over my childhood.

On July 18, 1990 I got to the MEPS station in Kansas City at 0600 or 6:00 am. I waited to be flown and bussed to USMC Recruit Depot in San Diego California. The bus picked up me and about 80 Marine recruits and took us to the airport at about 10:00 in the morning. We flew out of the airport and met with 60 more Marine Recruits in Denver at 3:00 pm from there we were on course to go to the Marine Corps Recruit Depot in San Diego.

Most of the recruits were pretty calm and talkative on the flight, but once we landed in San Diego the mood among the recruits changed very quickly. Kids were no longer just joking around. They were becoming very anxious about what to expect. We talked about how intimidating the Drill Instructors (D.I.s) would be, how would they act and what would be told to do. We had no idea of what to expect and there were so many stories and in fact there is a mythos surrounding the DIs but we had yet to experience one firsthand and had no idea of what was coming our way.

Around 8:00 pm PST (2000 hrs.) the busses from the Recruit Depot arrived to pick up about 300 wild eyed and highly anxious recruits. Drill Instructors were present along with other Marines. We were told to get in the busses one at a time but quickly so that we were almost on top of each other. There was no just two people to a seat. There were three and four wannabe Marine recruits to a seat with two more in the aisle and on the floor. The ride itself was short but a good introduction to what we would experience for the next three months. FYI, the USMC Recruit Depot in San Diego is adjacent to the San Diego Airport.

After that short fifteen-minute ride we arrived at the recruit depot. We were told to get off the busses in the same fashion as we got on them, A to B. We were then ordered to place our feet on the yellow footprints that were on the quarter deck.

While we were standing on the yellow footprints, all 300 of us, we were told what to expect for the next 13 weeks. What the Drill Instructors said was THE LAW! If they ordered, you to jump the recruit was to ask how high. If you were told to do something, you made the upmost effort to do it as quickly and precisely as possible. We were no longer just the children of our parents. We were now property of The United States Marine Corps.

The first thing done together as a company was get our heads shaved. We were told to form single lines and we waited to be instructed on when our line was to go. We waited and then we were sent in and once in we formed another single line with each recruit sitting with knees on the floor with each recruits' knees in the others back until the Barber directed us to take a seat, once in the Barber's chair you didn't have much of a choice as to what haircut you wanted. They said one thing to each recruit.

"If you got a mole or wart on your scalp point to it." This was done to avoid the bloody mess that could happen if the clippers met up with a wart. Otherwise, they just ran their clippers across your head and off your hair fell to the ground.

Once my head was shaved, back in line I went until the Drill Instructors told my line to come outside. I hesitate to say march because at that time only a few of the recruits had any concept of the idea. We were told to form up a "platoon" and we were sent to a temporary barracks where we could start our in-processing. We were given multiple tasks and busy work to perform until the morning. When morning arrived; we went to chow at 05:30 am. After chow, the Drill Instructors instructed us in basic marching skills otherwise known as drill. We then began our in-processing. This consisted of initiating medical and dental records as well as academic testing.

After approximately 36 hours without any sleep, we were re-administered the armed services vocational aptitude battery test. This was the same test all the recruits were given at their local MEPS station weeks or months earlier; only this time we were sleep deprived. Once we finished the test, we formed back up and continued with our other in processing matters under the watchful eyes of our temporary D.I.'s.

When we got back to our temporary barracks we were told to shit, shower and shave. All 100 of us did this squeezed into a bathroom meant for twenty people while butt naked. When I got done in the community shower, I took a minute to look up and noticed a strange reflection in the mirror. Never mind there were 99 other bald heads but there was one in the mirror that looked quite odd. Then I realized it was me. It seemed as though time stood still as I gazed into the mirror. I don't think I was the only recruit to have this reaction; however, I didn't notice anyone else taking a second to look up at the mirror. I quickly came to and started getting my things squared away for my first nights inspection and fire watch.

In this first week of bootcamp, we recruits learned to form into a platoon, march, and do the most basic of drill(marching). We also had a multitude of immunizations and shots that would rival any experimental test subject. Of course, as I mentioned before a battery of tests was thrown at all recruits. This was done to determine what special attributes of any if the recruits possessed. Special testing continued throughout boot camp for a few recruits with me included. For my part, special testing lasted through to the second month of boot camp. I did well enough between my test scores and linguistics testing to merit multiple sessions. However, I was not called back for special testing after our company's 24-mile hump with 80 lb combat load over Mount Mother in the second phase of boot camp.

In the first four weeks of boot camp recruits were humiliated, intimidated, subjected and disciplined. We were drilled relentlessly on the doctrine and history of the Marine Corps, as well. This was all done in an effort to mold recruits into a single-minded functional unit, or in other words, a team. I would be remiss to neglect the 05:00 am reveley every morning with the exception of the 06:00 am reveley on Sunday Mornings. Recruits were never so thankful for church service before.

Everyday we woke up with Drill Instructors screaming at us to get up, out of the rack and move faster. The goal was for us to be up and dressed as quickly as possible in our "boots and utes" in under two minutes. We were being taught to respond quickly under pressure and be precise and functional even first thing in the morning when most people are taking two minutes to wipe the sleep out of their eyes when they wake up. If you could get dressed in cammies and boots in two minutes time; two minutes seemed like an infinite amount of time in comparison as though you could accomplish just about any menial task in two minutes time. Speed and precision was the essence of Marine Corps Boot Camp.

We could be assured to run at least three miles in formation every day except Sundays. Marching in platoon formation or "close order drill" was done every day for what seemed a minimum of six hours. We studied Marine Corps history, philosophy and weaponry at least a couple of hours every day. There was little time for a recruit to have any down time. The down time that was afforded was between 2100-2200 (9:00 and 10:00 pm). In this hour we were told to shit, shower and shave. We were encouraged to write home to loved ones and any friends we may have. I spent a lot of time I had writing to family and the tight knit group of friends I had back home. It seemed when the nightly inspection. was called at 2200 hours it had never been enough and there I would be standing in my government issue olive green t-shirt and underwear awaiting the drill instructor to declare me fit to hit the rack and I would again, have an unfinished letter left for the next night. After the order was given to hit the rack I would desperately climb my bunk and within minutes after being given the order for lights out I would be asleep.

Firewatch was assigned to all members of the platoon by rotation. When it was your turn you hoped for either early or late. Either way it was dreaded. All in all, it didn't matter when you got it. Bootcamp was three months of sleep deprivation.

The next month of boot camp was dedicated to weapons and field training. A full two weeks was geared to learning how to fire the M-16 A2 service rifle with accuracy and precision. If you did not meet the Marine Corps standards for qualification you would be dropped from your platoon and stay behind in a marksmanship-training platoon until you got it right. Dropping a recruit from a platoon also happened in first phase; if a recruit could not pass the physical fitness test, recruits would be placed in the "Pork Chop Platoon" or physical conditioning platoon if the recruits just didn't measure up. If a recruit had an injury he would be left behind and placed in the physical rehabilitation platoon. When this happened to a recruit it meant more time in boot camp and that is the last thing any recruit wants, but it happened and happens in every platoon in bootcamp.

While at Recruit Field Training Depot at Camp Pendleton the first two weeks were spend working on PMI (Primary Marksmanship). Recruits were taught the basics of marksmanship by the Drill Instructors before beginning classes with the Primary Marksmanship Instructor who was a Staff Sergeant and one rank higher than our Drill Instructors and treated the recruits with a little more respect that did our benevolent Drill Instructors.

We learned how to shoot a small round disc in a target from 200 meters in the off-hand position. Good body mechanics are absolutely needed as well as excellent timing. In the off—hand position once you have the proper form and the front site tip is on the target you will notice the front site tip doing a figure eight around the center of where you have the rifle barrel placed. If you time the trigger squeeze just right and mechanics are good you just might hit that small black circle in the target or come very close which isn't necessarily bad either. The next range is 300 meters sitting and kneeling positions. After that we moved to the 500-meter line, shooting 10 rounds in the prone position. At that time, a score of 250 meant you hit all fifty targets in the center black area of the target.

I remember so many recruits being nervous about possibly not qualifying and having to stay back at the PMI course. That did happen, as we were shown a platoon of recruits who were dropped from their platoons because they did not qualify on their assigned weapon. I remember like it was yesterday, one of our Drill Instructors was taunting the recruits in the platoon. I was no exception to the taunting. We were all told we would fail and we would be dropped from our rotation. That is the last thing any recruit wants to hear because that means more time in boot camp. I believe after qualification day on Edison Range, all but one recruit from my platoon qualified. On that day I qualified as a Sharpshooter. One Step Below Rifle Expert which is what the Marine Corps prefers. I did eventually qualify as a Rifle Expert while in the Marine Corps, just not that time. I can also say with pride, I never qualified as a "pizza box" marksman. I was either a Sharpshooter or a Rifle Expert. My DD214 reflects that.

The final month of bootcamp A.K.A phase three was mainly a rehash of the first month with swim qualification added in. Oh joy! I was not a great swimmer. I was just glad I was able to tread water for 15 minutes with my gear shed and mostly with buoyancy staying on my backside. I passed the swim qualification.

There was again the incessant drill, Marine Corps traditions and guidelines, purchasing of uniforms and other sundry items in five minutes time. When graduation day came, on a warm Friday in October, I was proud, relieved, confident and concerned. I had just completed the introductory phase to service in not only the Armed Forces but The United States Marine Corps! I had an idea of what to expect but I wasn't at all certain of the road that lay before me.

My mother and Emily had come to witness my big day. William and Amanda were busy with their lives and did not attend. My father did not come either. I don't know if it was my father's fear of flying, his medication or something else, regardless he was not there. As so many times before, my father was absent. He had been missing from baseball games, football games, band competitions, high school graduation and now this. I once again had mixed feelings about the situation. I was glad my mom and sister were able to attend. I wasn't sure whether to be happy or upset.

I had now become a US. Marine. I was immensely proud and confident but once again I could not shake the awkwardness of the relationship with my father and his routine absence. He had not been around for a good deal of my childhood, but for a great deal of it, when he was at home it was not quality time. Rarely did my father spend time with me one on one. Often, I had been afraid of him. He never did take the time nor was he capable of assuaging my fear of him. The fact he had neglected to reach out to me is what hurt and left me feeling odd. Isn't this the sort of thing that causes aberrant behavior in young men? It happened to Will. Would it be in my nature to fall easy prey to manipulative women or drugs. Could it happen to me? It hadn't happened yet.

CHAPTER 11

Harshness and Sadness

I was now headed to the first iteration of Marine Combat Training. This addendum to training was designated for all Personnel Other Than Grunts (Marines not 0300 series) AKA P.O.G.S. It consisted of more weapons training, setting up fox holes, rappelling and live fire training. Of course, how could I forget but more humping/hiking up around Mount Mother again and running for a mile in full battle rattle. This all took place at San Ofreo near and on Camp Pendleton and lasted for a month.

Now, I feel the urge to correct a few things that Hollywood just will not ever seem to get right or properly capture in the current environment of the movie experience. When a hand grenade is thrown specifically, the M67 and M68 hand grenades which are ball shaped the impact could be considered overwhelming. Once you remove the safety pin from the grenade it is not yet armed. You may keep hold of the "spoon" on the grenade as long as you like but once you release the spoon on the grenade you should wait a couple of seconds and then throw the grenade which is extremely hard to do. Why is it hard you ask. Have you ever held an explosive in your hands that could kill or maim everyone within fifteen feet? The reason the grenade holder/thrower should wait, is due to the 5-7 second delay and the desire to avoid getting into a game of "Catch the Hand Grenade" with the enemy. A point that I'm trying to emphasize is that when a hand grenade such as the M68 detonates, it can be felt all around in a 100-yard radius shaking the earth. It is no little thing that simply breaks the windows. Realistically one could blow a large hole through a brick wall and could be felt throughout an entire neighborhood for example.

The other issue is the effect of suppressors on firearms in the military. Typically, military suppressors will bring the sound of a rifle shot to near 150 decibels or possibly a little lower. Mind you, 150 decibels is still well above the termed "Threshold of Pain" which is from 90-130 decibels. The movie industry and the mainstream media has worked hard to rename suppressors "Silencers". There is nothing silent about a 130 to 150 decibel sound! The whole purpose of a suppressor is to limit the "report" of the rifle or handgun which is the distance from which the sound of the suppressed rifle shot may be heard.

Once this month of extremely difficult and demanding remedial training was done, I was off to school for my primary military occupation specialty. (MOS) I was now a U.S. Marine. My schooling was nothing unusual. I learned the basics of music theory, music arrangement, ear training, as well as the perfunctory marching drill along with the rest of the other service men and women of other military branches.

The hardest task I had was learning how to play a second instrument. I was given 6 months to be as proficient on my second instrument as someone who had been playing on it for a number of years. Not an easy proposition for a young 18-year-old did man who wanted to see the world and have a little fun while on liberty. I did end spending about 15-20 hours a week at one-point learning how to play the guitar proficiently.

While I was at the school of music, I was often so busy I had hardly any time to think about my family back home. Our lives (Soldiers, Marines, and Sailors) were so structured that we had little time for a social life. We were required to spend a minimum of 10 hours a week on each instrument we were obligated to play. This was in addition to any rehearsal time which were involved in.

During the time I was stationed at Little Creek Amphibious Base, I received letters from friends, my siblings and of course my mom. Of all letters I received from loved ones, two specific letters from my mother stand out most in my mind.

The first of these two letters came around February that year. In short, what it said was that my Grandmother was trying to have my father declared non-compos mentis or rather mentally incompetent. According to my mother, my Aunt Laura (Licentious) was pushing my grandmother to pursue this action.

For years in the 1980s my father's family had been trying to sell 300 acres of land in the central Kansas area that our family farm had been on and all the while my father blocked the sale of the land. It was his livelihood. It was how he contributed to the support of his family. He did not want that stripped away from him. Who could blame him, schizophrenic or not?

My mother said in the letter that my grandmother was aggressively seeking for this declaration on my father, which would mean my father ultimately would not have any rights to make any decisions for himself regarding anything. Could you imagine not having the right to do some of the most basic things such as decide on your course of medical treatment, what car insurance you use, or the right to buy or sell real estate or other property; but this is what my grandmother wanted for her son, my father.

Well, a few months went by and I prepared for my final exams and recitals. I had spent countless hours practicing in small cubical practice rooms and I was ready to show my stuff to the instructors for the last time.

The day before my final recital I received the second of two letters from my mom. It stated that my grandmother had not been able to have my father declared non compos mentis as my father had lately been compliant with his meds and he had done well with the psychiatrists. However, my Aunt Licentious and my grandmother maneuvered and managed to get a power of attorney over my father. As a result, my grandmother and aunt had managed to get a buyer and sell the farm for one half the market value.

Consequently, my grandmother and aunt got the immediate money that my aunt had wanted but managed to cheat my father and my other aunt's family out of hundreds of thousands of dollars and guess who got control of all my father's share of the sell he never agreed to?

No, it was not my mother. It was my grandmother. She controlled every penny that my father had rights to. Once again, Aunt Licentious had done her worst.

The next day, after having a night to rest on the news, I was due to perform my recital and I did. I passed and the instructors praised my progress I made in just three months' time. I passed by the skin of my teeth. When I was done, I was relieved that the performances were behind me; however, things were starting to heat up with my family back home.

As with many times before in my life. I had mixed emotions. My grandmother had sold the land and had money, yet my family had so little to show for it. We had money, yet we had no money at all. Either way, my father and my immediate family lost what he had been trying to hold onto all those years. Incompetent or not, he was stripped by his own mother of his right to provide for his family while she held and controlled all that was gained from the sale of the land.

After the property was sold, my father retired permanently to his recliner. Maybe it was his medication that kept him so sedate. After all, Haldol has the reputation of being able to snow anybody under. But, I also feel my father's internal drive, his sense of motivation, was seriously hurt or even crushed when the farm was sold without his input. It was as though his sister and mother had neutered him and in so doing so stated that my father's voice was unnecessary and invalid.

That June, I was now on my way to my first duty station. When I got there the band was out of country and I was assigned to Battalion Police for my first assignment at my duty station. So, I picked up trash and cleaned up important people's offices for a few weeks. What an introduction to military life in the Marine Corps this was. It did get better though, much better.

When the band got back from their mission, I was introduced to the other Marines in the unit; and though I didn't realize it at the time, my future wife. It took about six months of practice, performances, physical conditioning and Thursday night field days (extremely thorough cleaning of the barracks) before we even spoke a word to each other aside from something critical such as your uniform is jacked up. But we eventually did speak to each other on a bus trip on the way to perform at a Marine Corps Birthday Ball Ceremony. A few months after that we began to date. When we did start dating, I found out I had competition from another Marine. I can remember waiting for her by her barrack's room door while she was out with this other Marine, who I felt was substandard and unworthy since he was married. That evening when she saw me waiting for her, she had a look of uncertainty in her eyes. She was visibly glad to see me but I think she was nervous because she had a feeling for what my intentions might be.

You must understand, like many young men with their first serious relationship, I had fallen head over heels for Lynn. She was funny, bright and fun to be around. She didn't seem to have any emotional baggage but then again, we were only 19 and 20 what baggage could she have? She knew I was serious about having a monogamous relationship with her and she was serious about me once she knew I was sincere. So many times, women are defensive and put up a wall against boyfriends for so many different things. They can't be held accountable for their small lizard brains which govern their mate picking. Lynn was no different, she had many previous boyfriends, more than I care to count. She'd been around but did not tell me that until later, much later.

After dating for several months, I proposed to her. Not how I wanted to propose to her but on her timeline because she wanted her parents to know we were engaged before we left New York. I had asked her father for his permission for Lynn's hand in marriage and he gave me his blessing. Six months later we were getting married.

My parents, Emily, Aunt Inge and my grandmother all flew up for the wedding. It was a small wedding with 100 or so guests. What mattered most to us was not the guest count but that we were getting married. The appearance of my Father was ironic to me. The man who had been missing from most of my formative years and who had been abusive in the time he was at home, was at my wedding and somehow, he did not miss this event. I'm not sure if his appearance was due to my mother's influence or if he took a plane ride to witness my marriage of his own accord. Either way, Michael was there to witness a major event of his son's life that day and to his credit, he did.

After Lynn and I had been married for a couple of years and our service time was up in the Marine Corps, we headed back to my home state of Kansas. We both optimistically began our pursuit of a college degree and adjustment to civilian life again. For Lynn, the adjustment may have been more difficult as she was now 1700 miles away from her family in New York. So not only did she have to adjust to the sometimes-oppressive heat of Kansas but also adjust to separation from home. She managed the adjustment pretty well with regular phone calls to Mom and Dad back home. We also flew up to New York on either Thanksgiving and Christmas and that trend continued for many years into the future.

I worked my way through college working 35-40 hours or more a week. Countless hours were spent studying and in Lynn's case practicing. She was a music major. She had decided to continue with the pursuit of some music related career. I had chosen the sciences and pursued a major in biology. We didn't have much of a social life but we did manage to find spare time for one another sporadically.

Early in my sophomore year in college I received a call from my mother. She had wanted to let me know that my grandmother intended to call a meeting between herself; my mother, myself and an attorney that represented my grandmother. The reason for this meeting was to discuss my father's legal situation regarding his mental status. Apparently, unbeknownst to me, my father had not yet been declared non-mentis compos and this meeting was another attempt for her to gain full control of the estate and place my father under "benevolent care". However, my grandmother had a rude awakening. Even her attorney did not believe it would be in my grandmother's best interest or our family's best interest to have this ruling on my father. You see my father would then be a ward of the state and have no rights at all. We were warned the next time he has a psychiatric admission nothing would prevent the state from moving him from one state facility to another as needed. Meaning we might not ever see him again, if or at the very least have a hard time locating him. Even the lawyer my grandmother had hired saw the injustice in this situation.

My grandmother didn't like this response, so she decided to fire him and sought out another lawyer's counsel. Amazingly enough, the next lawyer gave her the same advice to not seek non-mentis compos for my father. My grandmother had to be content with her power of attorney as though that was not enough to deprive my mother and our immediate family of what was ours all because an empty can was continually rattling regardless of what was given to fill it.

One day in late December of my Senior year in college I received a phone call from my mom telling me my father had been admitted to the hospital. At first, I thought nothing of it. He had been in and out of hospitals so many times before that this should be not earth shattering. But this time the hospital was for medical purposes not psychiatric. My father had been admitted for congestive heart failure and abnormal sinus rhythm. I went to the hospital to visit my father the next day. He was doing well. We talked about football, how I was doing in school, how Lynn was doing, etc. My father seemed in good spirits. I found out later on that day my father was scheduled for a pacemaker implantation early the next week.

Early the next week on Tuesday I received a call from my mother that I should head down to the hospital. I thought my mom's voice sounded stressed and urgent. It seemed a bit odd and unnecessary. I knew from my schooling that my father's congestive heart failure could be ameliorated through diuresis with Lasix or some similar diuretic to rid the body of excess fluid. The subject of the pacemaker implantation was a non-issue because that is to a cardio-thoracic surgeon as a tune up is to a mechanic. It wasn't complicated.

When I got to the area outside my father's room, I saw my mother and Emily. They were both in tears. I knew instantly something had gone wrong and indeed something had gone wrong. While my father was on the operating table, he had a massive heart attack and expired after more than an hour of CPR and advanced life support measures. I had seen my father for the last time and did not realize it until that instant. I was angry, I had lost my father and was angry at our family for what I had lost and been deprived.

My family spent the remainder of the day making calls and comforting one another. The next day was cluttered with funeral arrangements, bills and the execution of my father's will. I cried over my father's death. Not only for his loss but for what again had been lost and deprived. I can remember dropping off my application for graduate school early in the morning and hoping to avoid anyone in my department, luckily, I did. All the professors were on vacation, so I managed to avoid the questions and the reactions. I didn't want anyone other than my wife to see my feeling the way I did, even though I'm sure they would have understood.

Thanks to my Aunt Licentious my family had little more than barely enough money to cover the cost of the funeral and the reception. She had managed to siphon over 50% of my father's share of the sale of the family farm. At the age of some sixty years old, she had never stopped trying to fill her empty can that would never be filled. I guess she had been simply conditioned to do so. This lady had no mental disabilities, neither mental nor physical. Yet, she had managed to get welfare from the government for literally decades and as though that was not enough, she demanded more than her fair share because she blamed her grandmother for an unstable childhood. What a travesty. She had still not grown up.

CHAPTER 12

Release

My father had now been released from his poignant life on earth. We were now to deal with my grandmother and her protection of Aunt Licentious (Laura), the can that would never be filled she was and is a truly sad soul.

My Grandmother was well intended but would never make up for the inequities of life for her youngest daughter. Around 2003, my Aunt L had taken my grandmother's credit card and used it for a chance to go gambling. Aunt L just needed a vacation from her stressful life. She managed to run up a $10,000 bill on gambling, drinks, meals and whatever else in Las Vegas.

More recently Aunt L's daughter Flo talked about attending college and my grandmother gave her $5,000 to pay for her semester's tuition. Flo had promised that she would attend college but instead of taking the money to the bursar's office to enroll in school; instead, she took the money that was intended for her first semester in college and had a weekend of fun with her lesbian girlfriend. That money was gone with the wind. Granted this is not a whole lot of money but these events happened about 15 years ago when the cost of daily living was just a little bit cheaper. This event is just another example of bad behavior that has become all too common in today's society.

Aunt L later became my grandmother's health care proxy and was responsible for her health care. Unfortunately, not long after this my grandmother suffered a broken hip at the age of 94 and slowly became a "shut in". She isolated herself from her neighbors, stopped driving her car thereby severely limiting her social interactions at the grocery store, beauty shop and even church. Due to her increasing immobility, Aunt L was given control of Zelda's finances.

My mother had helped my grandmother by running errands, assisting her with bathing, cooking and other daily chores that had to be done around the house. My mother's continued assistance to her mother in-law lasted for about four years when my mom was not doing substitute teaching.

In 2006, Zelda, my grandmother passed away at the age of 96 and Aunt L became the executor of my Grandmother's estate which was still about 200 acres in the greater Kansas City area. When the highway came through and the government split the farm in two decades ago, this is what was left after the sell of the land in the late 1980s.

The real tragedy of this is not that this property is potentially valued being worth millions of dollars. Instead of this being seen as something to bring together the family it has done quite the opposite. It's worth of perceived value instead drove a wedge between the families. While two families see eye to eye and communicate with each other effectively, the other family fails to communicate with the other two families in a productive manner.

It is very likely due to greed and ill will between the families that this land may not sell andmay be lost to high property taxes. This may be a well-deserved fate for my extended family. Why in world would God reward such reprehensible behavior. However, the real estate market has little to do with Godly behavior. The fate of the property remains an unknown. It remains on the real estate market at this time near the end of the year. Though, due to so many unpredictable factors this year (2024), it's anybody's guess what could happen regarding anything.

My immediate family's hope, which is composed of Veterans such as myself, does not want the property sold to a purchaser from a foreign government. This desire or wish may become nothing more than a wish due to the impact of the COVID 19 phenomena to adversely affect the real estate market. What happens to the property remains to be seen at the time of writing.

As the months after my father's death passed by, I thought of him less frequently and with less pain. I was focused on graduating and gaining entrance to graduate school. The less I heard of and from my grandmother and Aunt Laura, the better off I felt I was. Thankfully, during that time I did not hear my mother complain about my grandmother or aunt at that time.

A year into graduate school I began my internship and Lynn began her internship as well. We met each other every other weekend for six months while she did her internship at the VA in Waco, Tx. My internship was in Ft. Worth, so we were separated by about 100 miles, just far enough away to prevent daily commuting.

We both managed to get through our internships in good condition. In fact, we were so successful that we were expecting our first child. The next nine months were not too different from what every other expecting parent knows, a mixture of anxiety and jubilation. Nothing was unusual. There were sonograms, Ob/Gyn visits, room preparation, etc. that were done. On March 10th at 3:10 pm Andrea Grace Magnusson was born. She was a healthy beautiful baby of 7 lbs. and 13 oz and 20 inches in length.

When I held that precious child for the first time, I was awash with a wave of illumination. I knew that at one time my father had to have felt the same love for me as I felt for that little angel. You see, Michael must have loved Sigmund and all his other children after all.

One year later, Lynn and I had a second child, Michael Robert Magnusson. This child looks exactly like his grandfather. He was a robust child at 8 lbs. and 14 oz and 21 inches. I was overjoyed and yet sad at the same time. Michael never got the chance to see these grandchildren or maybe he did? Regardless of what happened now with Licentious (Laura) and my grandmother, it just didn't matter. Lynn and I had made it on our own, so would our little family no matter what it took, because a responsible parent does what needs to be done to provide for their children.

CHAPTER 13

Unforgettable

Wouldn't you know that after I earned my master's degree, I moved to upstate New York with my wife and two small children at the end of Y2K. I began working at a medium sized hospital in upstate NY that has since been renamed. In an effort to pay bills and provide for a family in a state with a higher cost of living I took on a part time job as a personal trainer at Gold's Gym in the local area.

My first jolt from the move to New York was the price of housing. We had moved from a 1400 square foot home in Kansas with two bathrooms and a garage with a price tag of $65,000 to a 1200 square foot home with one bathroom and no garage for a price of $120,000 in Upstate NY.

I can honestly tell you all the medical personnel, staff, personal trainers and people in general that I worked with and lived by, were by and large welcoming people. They were and I'm sure still are hardworking people just trying to provide for their families just like so many other people do in America.

In our first summer in New York state, we visited places like Sleepy Hollow, The Vanderbilt Mansion and Vanderbilt Estate, The Culinary Institute of America, and other noteworthy places when we had free weekends and time off.

When the summer ended the children began day care and my wife began her job in sales for a wireless company. The quality of day care was good but just like everything else in upstate NY the cost of childcare was high at $1200 for our two young children per month. The cost of childcare gave me the incentive to continue my part time job. At this point, I was working about 60 hours a week between my full-time job at the hospital and personnel training.

Another odd event happened in my life about this time. Early that first summer in Upstate NY, Lynn and I had brought our two young children to see their grandparents and have dinner that evening. We were having a great time joking with Joe and Ronnie. Then a couple of hours into the evening I received a call from my oldest sister Amanda. She had called to me with urgency to tell me that Emily had just attacked our mother. Emily had bit her causing bleeding and hit her several times causing bruising.

Our mother had gotten scared enough that she called 911. Emily had now been arrested for elder abuse. You see our mother was 67 years of age. They may have also charged her with domestic violence but I'm not sure of it. It was so sad and so shocking to hear that my older sister, who I was proud of, and was a graduate of Rice University had let her emotions about a breakup with a boyfriend overwhelm her and she apparently lashed out at our mother. My sister spent a night in jail and was given deferred adjudication.

It was a first-time offense and Emily received leniency from the court. I was concerned that Emily may have a similar psychiatric disposition similar to our father because she had definitely been violent and was too demanding and demeaning to our mother who was always bending over backwards to help her.

What was Mom's repayment. Assault and abuse. She had seen enough of that type of abuse from my father and now she was getting it from Emily. I felt guilty, as though I had let my mother down, even though I was roughly 2,000 miles away. What could I have done? Could I have intervened? Would it have made a difference. It did not matter. My mom had suffered enough abuse and I felt she should not have to endure anymore. I knew I could not allow something like this happen again.

At the beginning of August, I had purchased tickets for my wife's 31st birthday to see Phantom of the Opera off of Broadway in New York City for her late September birthday. She just loved Broadwaymusicals but I could only afford Off Broadway prices.

On a beautiful strikingly blue-sky late summer morning I reported to work at 8 am and began prepping the paperwork for the patients I needed to see, assist and assess that day. Around 8:45 a.m. I made my way up to the 5th floor of the hospital and began doing my rounding of patients on the floor and charting. Then sometime around 9:15 a.m. I hear someone shouting from the day room on the floor that a plane just flew into one of the twin towers.

All the nurses, doctors, and other medical staff as well as I turned toward the person who blurted that jaw dropping expression out as though we could not believe our ears and we could not believe what we were hearing. What Erin the Physical Therapist was saying was utterly unbelievable. My first thought was it was probably some little Cessna that had gotten of course. I thought this because not too long before a small plane had crashed into some of the buildings in the city. Then a minute later I heard that it was an American Airlines jet that had struck one of the towers. Then another minute later we heard that the other tower had been hit by a similar size jet. This seemed unbelievable.

Hours went by, I continued like everyone else in the U.S to try and wrap my head around what was going on. I immediately thought of the report from around 1998 that President Clinton had missed that terrorist in the middle east. I could not think of his name, but I knew he was tied to the attempted Twin Towers bombing 1993. Then not too long after that I was getting back on the elevators to go up to the 5th floor again and an older gentleman was getting off the elevator and he looked at me and my coworker and said, "I just know it was Bin Laden" . Joan and I just looked at each other in astonishment.

A few days later was September 20th my wife's birthday. My In-laws, my wife and I were headed down to see Phantom of the Opera off Broadway. We took the rail from upstate NY down to Grand Central Station which took about two hours' time. Once we exited Grand Central Station, we walked many blocks toward the Manhattan area. As we got closer, we could see there was no more Twin Towers on the skyline and the city was so full of dust, rubble and trash. This was 9 days after 9/11 and people were still very nervous about what had just happened and rightfully so. But as all the Thespians would say,"The show must go on" and it did. My wife and her parents were happy, at least temporarily so.

Even though, we were about a mile and a half from ground zero the effects of the event could be seen and nearly were palpable in most New Yorkers as you passed them by in the street. This had been a profound life altering event and all of America would soon learn that their way of life would be inexorably changed in countless ways all due to the acts of terrorism in NYC and Washington D.C. It was also the last time we would see all of our Senators and Congressman from all parties coming together on our Capitol steps in a show of unity and singing God Bless America.

Shortly, in a few weeks, we would hear about Special Forces making their way into Afghanistan to strike back at Al Qaida, the perpetrators of the 9/11 attack. We did not know it at the time, but Afghanistan would become a base of operations in the war against terror with hundreds of thousands of Soldiers, U.S. Marines and Sailors rotating through the many F.O.B.s (Forward Operating Bases) that were on six month or 1-year rotation schedule for the next twenty years.

In the Spring of 2002, being a patriotic and proud American, I called a Naval Recruiter and inquired about the Navy's Medical Officer program. I had several interviews with Naval Officers, went to M.E.P.S. and passed the physical. I filled so many forms and various paperwork that was required as well as recommendation letters and my DD214 from the Marine Corps.

I spoke with one Naval Captain, which is the same rank as what the USMC and Army call Full Bird Colonels, and she seemed to love the fact that I had been in the Marine Corps. Then after all my paperwork had been submitted I received a call from a Naval Commander (rank equivalent to a Lieutenant Colonel) that my application for Naval OCS had not been approved. I was dumbfounded. I had a master's degree. I was in better than average physical condition for my age and I had an intense desire to serve once again. I could not figure out why I was denied by the Navy, for all its wisdom, the Navy was not going to give me any clues.

So, there it was, I was going to continue working in upstate NY. I would continue to watch on the nightly news the events unfolding in Afghanistan, and I was not in uniform serving our country. My period of Veteran status continued for another year.

In 2003 the US. Armed Forces invaded Iraq and in February I began the enlistment process in The New York National Guard serving one weekend a month and did so for the next year. While in the New York National Guard, my unit was sent to Bamberg, Germany to serve for a few months in relief of the Big Red 1 (1st Infantry Division) while the active-duty unit we were serving in place of the unit that was down range in Afghanistan. Incidentally, it was one of the hottest summers on record in Bamberg and all of Europe was experiencing a heatwave at that time. I remember being on liberty one afternoon and when myself and couple of other Soldiers went to the PX (Post Exchange) it was so hot we all jumped in the beer cooler.

That may sound strange, but the beer cooler was so large it was a walk-in cooler the size of the dairy section at a Sam's Club or Costco. It was big and cool and very comfortable at a chilly temp of 10 degrees centigrade.

The outside temperature that day was 100 degrees Fahrenheit/38 degrees Celsius. Mind you, there are no air conditioners in Europe, for the most part, and there definitely weren't any on that military post and definitely not in that PX. Freiheit temp for all the children in Germany.

After my unit returned from Germany a few months went by and I decided to start the application process for a commission in the U.S Army Reserves. I filled out the paperwork, application packet, submitted my transcripts and other necessary information.

In April of 2004 I got the word from my Army Recruiter that the board at Human Resources Command for the Army in St. Louis, Missouri had approved my packet pending my physical and security clearance. After going through M.E.P.S now the fourth time and passing my physical now at 34 years old would be a 1st Lieutenant in the Army Medical Specialist Corp pending my security clearance and attendance at Officer Basic Course at Fort Sam Houston, Texas.

Unfortunately for Lynn, her father passed away from pancreatic cancer that same year in the fall. You would have never known in 2001 that Lynn's father Joe had anything wrong with him. He wasn't necessarily the picture of health but he wasn't unhealthy either. It's worth noting the Joe had smoked for over twenty years and did quit in his forties. He also took acetaminophen like candy for his chronic back pain. Joe's illness just came on rather suddenly and I know it was a terrible shock to her family. However, Lynn has rose-colored glasses and was not terribly shook up when Joe did pass away 11 months later. She simply said he was better off now and with the Lord. I agreed with that sentiment but still never saw her shed a tear. Which just seemed unusual. However, I did not push the matter with her and let her grieve in her own way.

Around the same time, I was commissioned a 1st Lieutenant in the U.S. Army Reserves and soon after that I attended Officer Basic Course at Ft. Sam Houston and of course Camp Bullis. It was a rather uneventful but an extremely informative time. I have to say that I was definitely reassured and inspired by the number of all my fellow classmates who had elected to join the military. My faith in America was renewed by all my fellow officers, who so many of which, were prior military service and were prior enlisted such as myself.

I must tell you about our afternoon on the firing line. It was duck and cover with one group of female medical officers who were nurses. They felt the M9 (Beretta 92) was a purse accessory or something that they could just swing around from side to side and one hand to the other. All of us who were prior enlisted, ran for cover because we knew to always treat a firearm as if it were loaded when it is on the firing line. The Range Officer came over and he promptly instructed the female officers on how to handle a firearm on the firing line. Many of the other fellow Officers were very grateful for the Range Officer's timely instruction.

While in the field we covered land navigation (map reading), communications with field radios, mounted and dismounted and of course first aid in the battlefield as well as other relevant topics. Before we could graduate, we all took our physical fitness tests. The average age of my classmates was about 40. The youngest probably was probably twenty something and the oldest was a gentleman that had to be at least 70 and was a psychiatrist. Yes, the Army needs them.

After I graduated from Officer Basic Course, I headed back to Upstate NY. Later that month we sold our house for a tidy profit and due to a stroke of luck and the housing bubble getting bigger but not bursting before we sold. It had only been on the market for about three months.

We were then headed back to Kansas where there was a lower state income tax and life is just more affordable in general. On the way down, we took our two children to Disneyworld and had a wonderful time. We also made the terrible mistake of buying a timeshare, which haunts me to this day.

When we got to my mom's house in July after our trip to Disneyworld, we saw that my mom was not in the best of health and was often dealing with shortness of breath. Shortness of breath in the Kansas heat is nothing unusual but while my 70-year-old mother was gently walking from the kitchen to her couch in a 76-degree air cooled house and was experiencing shortness of breath I knew something was not quite right.

She had been seeing a cardiologist and she was referred to a cardiothoracic surgeon to have open heart surgery in August. She had failed to reveal this to me until she needed a ride to the Doctor's office. Later that month she had a Quintuple bypass of her coronary arteries. She was in the ICU then the PCU for a total of a week and was then sent to rehabilitation for strengthening and conditioning after surgery.

In September she was discharged home for recovery. Her discharge plans were simple, as Lynn and I were there to help mom out. Lynn and I were both looking for work at the time, since our move, so one of us was always at home to assist my mom as needed at that time.

I was just so glad at the time that our 70 plus-year-old my mom had made it out of a grueling five-hour surgery in relatively good shape considering her age. I felt things were looking up for my mom and my family.

CHAPTER 14

You Wouldn't Know (BÜCK DICH)

While my mother was still recovering from her surgery, Lynn and I discovered we needed just a little more room for our clothes in the closet while we stayed temporarily with my mom. Mom suggested we call Emily and ask her to remove some of her coats, dresses and other clothes that were packed from side to side and top to bottom in the closet that was in the room we were in.

Emily came by a few days later at my mom's house asking us what we thought we were doing and why were we bothering her. I simply explained to her that we just needed some room for our own clothes in the closet, however, Emily did not seem to want to help at all. Instead, she started yelling at me and telling me how sorry I was staying at mom's house with my kids.

I tried to get Emily to calm down because our mom was still recuperating from her open-heart surgery and our mother needed her rest. I just wanted to prevent Emily from agitating our mother as Emily so seemed to enjoy doing. The last thing we did not need and definitely did not want was for Emily to assault someone again. I endured about ten minutes of Emily insulting me, my wife and my children before I managed to draw her out to the kitchen where the entrance for the garage door was.

I pleaded with Emily to calm down and to please leave us in peace. For whatever reason, she had no intention of doing what any normal or polite person would do. Instead, she refused to leave and continued shouting at me and insulting my wife and two small children. She was just being truly ugly. I threatened to call the police but she failed to budge. She remained by that door taunting and threatening me.

I attempted to open the door and Emily blocked me and struck at me. She was hitting my neck. When she did that, I forcibly moved her and as I began to move her, she started hitting at me more, scratching and kicking me. She managed to leave scratches on my neck and bruises on my shin, but I did get her out of the house. I managed to hit the garage door opener and get the garage door open. When I hit the garage door opener I made sure to push her away from the control so she couldn't stop the door from opening and so the neighbors could see her ugliness. When the door opened, she ran away. I was glad to see her leave. We still did not have any space in the closet and she had just been incredibly nasty. I then just felt so incredibly sorry for my mother. I now had an idea of the lunacy she had been putting up with before Emily got married and left the house. Emily was no longer the sister that I remembered but someone that had completely changed.

You see A few years earlier Emily started a relationship with a fellow teacher who was a teacher of art or so he claimed. You see Donald had knocked up Emily a few months before their wedding in 2002 and he had an aura about him that just made people want to turn and walk away. Ronald was a very smug man and had not one ounce of humility or much respect for his fellow man. He was a short, bearded and heavy-set man with a protruding abdomen. I just thought; how could any chick, much less my sister hook up with this dude? But in fact, she did, further evidence of Emily's lunacy.

About thirty minutes after the scuffle with my sister, Donald calls my mother while she's resting and asks for me. I than obliged my mom and answered Donald's phone call. Donald asked me," Where do you want the police to pick you up? Do you want them to arrest you at home or at work?" I then replied. to Don," Do you even know what happened?" He then replied, "I know enough". I tried to explain to Donald what had happened. He would hear none of what I had to say. To which I replied, "Goodbye, Asshole!" and hung up the phone. I just thought this is great my career as an officer is over!

Donald simply was acting as the jerk he is, rendering judgement without knowing all the facts. It was just his character, and it has not changed to this day. This man will never have true friends.

The next day I went to my temporary workplace and waited for something to happen. Days went by at work. At my mom's house, I was never served a warrant or given a notice concerning the incident with Emily. Months went by and nothing happened. I just thought that figures. Ronald was just full of hot air and had not actually pursued charges or had no grounds to pursue charges as he had not been an actual witness.

I began drilling with a unit in Kansas as a Reservist and sought out counsel from the J.A.G. and they told me my rights and as the event in question did not happen while I was on active duty the Army Reserves could not pursue charges but if anything did happen, I was to let the civilian court system do their job if it came to that. I said thank you Captain and I saluted him as I left his door. I was relieved somewhat but I just knew this situation was not over. I just had that feeling that something wasn't quite right.

I had been looking for a better job in Wichita, but I couldn't make it past the first interview at several places that I had interviewed. I couldn't figure out what was going on but something was going on. I then started looking at jobs outside of my hometown and I came upon a couple of opportunities in East Kansas. I did the research, and I pursued both jobs. I needed a decent job to support my familyafter all.

The first interview, I did not like the feel of the company and some of the employees gave me a bad vibe. It seemed like some of the employees at that hospital were tweaking, high on methamphetamine. That hospital was immediately scratched off the list. The next week I was prepping for the next interview. It was a little further away and had previously been part of the Catholic Hospital System like the hospital I had been at in Upstate New York, and I liked the feel this hospital. No tweakers could be seen. At least they could not be seen yet.

I interviewed with the Director and the Chief of Services, and the interview went very well. I developed a good rapport with both gentlemen in a matter of minutes. After about twenty minutes of an interview, I was hired. I told Lynn and she was happy. I felt hopeful.

A few weeks later I was contacted by the hospital to come in for a drug test. While I was there, I was told by one of the employee nurses in human resources I had a warrant for my arrest per my background check. I honestly said to the nurse" I have no idea what it's about". I then realized what had happened. I then realized that asshole Donald had done what he threatened to do. I told Lynn and she was just astounded. I was feeling less hopeful at this point.

That April, on my birthday on a cold rainy evening I returned to my mom's home near to visit and called the police station to turn myself in. The police came and picked me up and I told the Officer what the situation was about, and he said," So, it is a, he said she said case". To that I said, "Yes sir, it is. Nobody saw what happened but Emily and I but I was accused by someone who wasn't even there". He said alright and placed me in cuffs.

I asked how long he had worked for the local PD and we had pleasant conversation up to the police station where I was booked like a common criminal. I stripped down to my birthday suit. I had to show the palms of my hands and soles of my feet, bend over and show the crack of my ass as though I was going through some sort of physical. I thought, what could somebody put up there? But I knew better. I felt violated. This was nothing like my Marine Corps experience it was the polar opposite. It was utter humiliation without redemption. When the police officer who brought me in handed me over to the booking officer, he said in a loud voice," THAT MAN IS GETTING SCREWED!"

After waiting in the jail cell for 6 hours I was finally released on a $500 bail bond. I had been charged with domestic violence and was now lumped in with all wife beaters. I had not placed charges on Emily for her assault on me because I didn't see what good it would do. I was now in the hand of the criminal courts.

A few weeks later I met a lawyer. This lawyer who was recommended was not very helpful as he did not even seem to try to put the situation in context but instead singularly focused on the fact that I had pushed my sister out of the way. My defense lawyer keyed in on that like it was some sort of severe crime. It's all he could talk about, and he strongly advised me to not go to trial and said If I didn't agree to a deal, I would likely be convicted and spend a year in jail. I just thought what type of a justice system is this where the defense lawyers are like this and are considered good. I felt like I should go to trial but my family Lynn and my mom told me not to go to trial. I eventually agreed to the plea deal and attended anger management every other week in the evenings driving 100 miles one way from where I lived for two months. Once I completed that course, the case was dismissed. However, I was advised that a Misdemeanor A would stay on my record would stay on my record unless it was expunged. He also said I had a good chance for expungement as I had no prior record. I couldn't help but think that what the Cop who arrested me said was so true. I was getting screwed while Ronald and Emily continued to take advantage of my elderly mother. They did manage to continually bilk my mother for the next 7 years until Emily eventually did what she does again. So, in essence the State of Kansas became complicit in allowing elder abuse to occur for the next 7 years.

On the positive side of things, I still for the moment had a good job and great home with property but now a criminal record courtesy of one smug son of a bitch and a bipolar sister and a flawed and rigged justice system. Mental illness is a real motherfucker and leaves no one in its proximity untouched. So, Emily gifted her brother who had earned his way in life a criminal record. What a sister.

I was later told by Bill the Director that I was still hirable but to let the court system play out. He oddly, did not seem too bothered by it. I thought that was a little odd, but I was like I really have a job and went with it. Lynn and I began looking at houses in the area and that Spring we bought our third house but now with 20 acres of land. I couldn't get that in New York for a million dollars and got it in the Kansas area for less than $200,000.00. Wow!

I continued drilling with my unit in the K.C area. It was war time, and the Army needed troops for all sort of missions that were happening in the states and around the globe. I was glad to be part of it but always had that situation with my sister and asshole brother-in-law in the back of my head. My security clearance had passed before the whole situation had happened and was good for ten years.

A couple of years later I was promoted and took command of a medical unit. About the same time my record came up for expungement and the crime of "domestic violence" was expunged a month later. That was critical because of the Lautenberg Amendment which negatively impacts anyone in the military or law enforcement. Basically, any job which may require the use of a firearm, you become ineligible to perform because of the Lautenberg Amendment. The expungement relieved me of that burden. I could now take my Company of Soldiers to a firing range without concern that I was violating any Army regulation. Talk about awkward.

I also had the distinct misfortune of having an extremely subversive and at times insubordinate First Sergeant who was active guard and showed disdain to all officers. She would have been all too happy to turn me into the Battalion Commander or Sergeant Major if she could. I was a Commander who led by example during training just as I had been taught in the Marines. You do it first and show the Troops how to do the task or assign the appropriate Subject Matter Experts to teach the task and be an active participant in training with the troops to foster good teamwork and camaraderie.

That First Sergeant of mine could not ever be seen during physical training. I counseled her on this matter many times and she would retort each time that "I'm on a profile." To which I would retort each time," exercise within your profile". I would tell her "The Troops need to see you out there with them and myself. She absolutely hated me because I held her feet to the fire and made her do her job. I had many times, advised the Sergeant Major when she was not. This experience was frustrating to say the least.

The Reserves are a little different, no, a lot different from active duty. That's not to say there aren't good Soldiers in the Reserves because there are many excellent Soldiers in the Reserves. However, due to the nature of training once a month and being civilians the remainder of the month a lot more leeway is afforded Soldiers due to exceptions to monthly training (drill) such as work conflicts or family needs so an example might be how they are afforded a different time in the month to make up the training that they missed and they would be supervised by full time staff. On active duty, if you didn't make it to training you were charged as absent without leave and sent for non-judicial punishment or something similar and strictly administrative but equally hurtful. A Reservist on active duty is bound by all the restraints and the same UCMJ (Uniform Code of Military Justice) so when mobilized, deployed or just on annual training they are held to the same standards as their active-duty counterparts.

While I was still in Company Command, we were on training in South Dakota and on the last day my S4 Officer (Logistics) Shawanda Williams told me that a male senior NCO (Non-Commissioned Officer) was seen sleeping with my First Sergeant who incidentally was married to another man I knew to be a Master Sergeant in another unit and by all accounts he was a good man. All I could do was shake my head as we gathered up all our gear and headed back to Kansas after a month of training. What a piece of work my First Sergeant was turning out to be. I said nothing of what I was told about to my First Sergeant, ever.

However, a few months later she did not like the NCOER (Evaluation Rating for NCOs) I gave her which was a fair rating but not a glowing review of her year's work as she had demanded. She demanded a sit down with the Battalion Commander, Sergeant Major and myself. Somehow, she had twisted the Sergeant Major's elbow and he was now demanding that I cut Lynette some slack. I persisted to the Lieutenant Colonel that she had not once in the past three years qualified on her assigned weapon with the troops and she had not ever taken a physical fitness test with the troops.

The Sergeant Major assured me that she would qualify on her weapon on the next qualification day. I knew this was not possible as I was responsible for the training calendar and my whole company had just qualified on their assigned weapons a few months earlier. I stood my ground and said I would not change my rating.

I should have expected what came next. I was served an I.G. (Inspector General) complaint from Lynetta. She claimed that I was both racist and sexist. I went through several rounds of interviews with the I.G.'s representative. All the senior NCO's and other Soldiers and Officers were questioned about my behavior. The interviews went on for about three months and the interviewing Captain who had previously informed me as soon as I met her, she informed me that her rank predated mine by a couple of months and was therefore senior to me told me when she was done with her interviews and she provided my Battalion Commander with a preliminary report.

One question from the interviewing Officer that I was very intrigued by was questioning my knowledge of an extra marital affair between the Sergeant Major and Lynetta my First Sergeant. I said I did not know of any affair. However, this made me think that Shawanda had told someone about what she saw In South Dakota and may have seen it on more than just that occasion. I, however, did not see it first hand and all I had was here say.

I was Informed by my Battalion Commander to not ask any questions regarding the investigation. He told me a few weeks later that no news is good news. LTC Martinez was an excellent Officer and was a Soldier's Soldier. At the age of 55 he was still running two miles in less than 16:00 minutes, performing 80 sit ups in two minutes and 60 pushups in two minutes for his physical fitness test. He too had been active duty and had been in the Army Airborne before going into the Reserves. He had my respect and I suspect he knew what was really going on but kept things functional as best he could. You see he was also a military technician and was at the unit full time during the month. He knew and agreed with me when I said Lynetta was subversive, insubordinate and unfit for her position but he also relayed to me because she was Active Guard Reserve, she would not be punished but eventually moved.

A few months later an opportunity for a deployment with a National Guard Unit to Camp Cropper in Baghdad became available for my skill set. I volunteered to go. I was emailing the Company Commander of the unit I would be deploying with what my situation was and tried to keep him informed of my availability. After a month of back and forth the National Guard Unit's Company Commander told me I was off the mission as an element of their mission at Camp Cropper had changed.

I would not know for several months why I was off the mission, but the day had come for Lynetta to PCS (Permanent Change of Station) or in other words move! It was also an exciting time for me as I had orders for a mobilization to Alaska. It turns out someone had noticed my willingness to volunteer for a mission overseas and I was rewarded with the Arctic Tundra!

I was placed as an Officer in Charge (OIC) of my section as I was no longer a Company Commander and was serving with the active Army. I felt extremely privileged to be where I was in spite of the sub-zero weather and being such a long way away from my wife and children.

The Soldiers I worked with were outstanding individuals for the most part with few exceptions. In every organization in military transgressions against other individuals or fellow Soldiers will happen even though every Command strives to maintain Soldier Discipline and keep this from happening.

I was tasked with ensuring all the Soldiers on post were adequately taken care of in the field and the hospital. I traveled to all over Alaska from one military base/post to another in order to assist Soldiers on the weight control program. Yes, I was driving from 100 to 200 miles monthly in the winter months at 30 degrees below zero or colder to make sure Soldiers at various Posts were taken care of just as the previous OIC in my position was tasked with doing.

I was tasked with Line of Duty assignments and other additional duties while stationed there. It was a busy and fulfilling year that I look back on with great fondness. I had a wonderful NCOIC (Non-Commission Officer in Charge) Sergeant First Class Parnell and his assistant NCOIC Staff Sergeant Dobbins. I would also often joke with a jab with another former US Marine turned Soldier. Specialist Bodet. He had been in the infantry and had seen action in Fallujah with the Marines and in Mosul with the Army with SSG Dobbins. I could not have been any more privileged than to be with those wonderful Soldiers.

One day, on the way to a weekly meeting with the Commander's Assistant, Sergeant Dugan told me about how her and Captain Woolsey had closed down the division I would have been working with at Camp Cropper under Big Army's Directive. Then I knew the answer why I did not deploy to Baghdad. Once again, I found myself fortunate to know the answer to a question I might otherwise have never known if Sgt Dugan had not been transferred to my section in the middle of the cold dark Alaskan Winter on a cold evening in December.

When my year was up at the Post in the middle of the Alaskan frontier, I was given recognition by the Army for all that I had done in the past year. I made sure to thank SFC Parnell and SSG Dobbins for all their hard work making our job accomplished. I could not have asked for better Soldiers. I made sure the Colonel in charge knew it. He definitely did understand my appreciation of my Soldiers once I was done speaking to the Troops.

A few weeks later my household goods were packed up from my bachelors' officer quarters I cleared the post and began my trip down the ALCAN, otherwise known as the Alaska Canada Highway. The last Soldier I saw before I left was Sergeant Dugan. She said," Goodbye, sir and good luck. Tear, tear as she motioned as though a tear drop was going down her cheek. I gave her a hug and said good luck to her and her husband. I made a similar motion of a tear drop going down my cheek and made my way off the Post.

While getting on the ALCAN 100 miles past Fort Greely I witnessed to a herd of caribou crossing the road. I slowed down and stopped to watch them pass. Sgt Dugan immediately came to mind. Tears began flowing down my cheeks because I knew I would never see those wonderful Soldiers again nor the beauty of the most beautiful state I have ever been privileged to be stationed in.

I traveled 10 hours a day for the next seven days traveling through the Alaska and the Yukon on day one. Day 2 was the Yukon. Day 3. British Columbia. Day 4 Alberta. Day 5 Montana and Yellowstone. I tried to get my wife to fly up and meet me with the kids in Yellowstone. Lynn however, had differentplans and felt it would be too much trouble and the kids had tests.

The next day's travel was through Idaho by misdirection, Wyoming, Colorado, Kansas (everybody loves my home state of Kansas). When I got back home Lynn, and the kids were gone and no one was at the house. My dog Max was the only being there to welcome me home and even he looked at me oddly. Lynn a few weeks later claimed I was being distant from the children. It is not abnormal for a Soldier who has been separated from his family for a long period of time to be having what the military calls reintegration problems or in civilian terms, trouble fitting back in. It also might be true that Lynn was being distant from me for some unexplained reason.

I was given 30 days by the Army Reserves to reintegrate and rejoin a unit. When I returned, I moved from the unit I had previously been responsible for standing up before my mobilization to a unit that was too large and had many problems with accountability partly because there was too much Brass in the unit (Too many Officers). This unit too had good Soldiers and, in my section, but were overlooked for promotion due to some strange reason I still can't discern.

Later that year, I was sent to a school that was necessary for promotion. I learned there what I should have learned prior to my command time. I learned things that my pre command course did not cover. Part of what I knew as a Company Commander was that you can plan and plan and plan some more but once your troops get in the field and start doing what they've been taught and trained to do they can either perform as trained or not perform due to poor training, poor retention of taught material or some unknown factor throwing a monkey wrench in things. The course I attended, emphasized using multiple courses of action to implement plans and mitigations for plans that go astray. I found it to be extremely helpful. When my class graduated, my wife met me with our children, and we had a good time in the local area prior to heading back to Kansas.

A month later I was back at my unit, and we were doing as we always did with our real-world mission and always under the gun by the Battalion Commander to perform our mission as all the enlisted Troops relied on us. Typically, our Battalion Commander was appreciative of our efforts but one thing that always irritated me was that my Troops were never recognized in my section in front of the formation no matter how many award recommendations I submitted. This made me feel demoralized for the troops. I have no doubt it was demoralizing for them as I saw many reach their ETS (End of Time in Service) and did not re- enlist.

My job at the hospital I was at was going well. I had received a promotion and just had the great privilege of hiring a former Full Bird Colonel from the Active Army (Many years retired) into a staff position. What a great addition and opportunity to learn.

That previous year my wife Lynn had gone into the Air Force National Guard after I had paid a $5,000.00 debt repayment after she left the Army National Guard without fulfilling her contract. She then decided to open a dance studio in town. She thought by operating as a nonprofit so she could make it work. She may have thought with our combined Reserve Pay we could make it work. It did not. Every month my Reserve pay was being used to pay the bills for her studio. She could not get enough operating revenue to pay the rent and utilities. In fact, most months she was not able to pay forty percent of her total rent bill for the space she was using. Unfortunately, this became a point of contention between the two of us. Within a year Lynn was forced to close the studio due to expensive rent and operation costs that had increased from the previous year. Even though I had been promoted at work received a raise it just was not enough to afford without sacrificing our house or something for our kids. Lynn had trouble dealing with the loss of her studio. I believe she blamed me. However, I certainly, wasn't telling people not to go to her studio. I was doing just the opposite. It's always easier to blame someone else rather than accept responsibility for your own actions. This is exactly the opposite of what the military teaches about accountability.

The translation of BÜCK DICH is literally get bent or bend over.

CHAPTER 15

ITBI

I was in for some good news provided by HRC Ft. Knox earlier that year I had been promoted in the Army Reserves. I was very proud of being able to achieve that rank having been enlisted previously. It was a big deal. I remember fondly of a fellow Soldier teasing me and opening the door for me after my name had come out on the promotion list. I was quite happy. Oddly though, Lynn did not make the effort to come to my promotion ceremony. I thought that was a bit odd and tried not to think about it too much.

Not more than a month after my promotion my sister Emily had some sort of emotional breakdown blow up or explosion. Maybe she had all three because she went apeshit all over our mother. Emily for some reason beat our mother again, throwing her down on the floor while punching and kicking the now 79-year-old woman.

I was called at work and informed of what happened. I drove 200 miles to Emily's house that our mother had bought for Emily and where our mother was staying. I found my mom still laying on the floor in sad condition. It was heart wrenching. After she was taken to the ER and X rays were performed it was revealed that my mom had sustained a concussion and three broken ribs from her daughter's fit. When my mom's condition was determined the Police were notified and came to take my statement as my mom was incapacitated and could not speak for herself at

95

that time. I relayed to the Policewoman everything my mom had told me about the assault as best as I could gather from my mom's garbled speech. I think the X-rays did more to convince the Police of what had happened than I could have ever done.

This was one of the most unpleasant things I had to do. I knew Emily had done something awful but I did not enjoy informing the Policewoman about Emily's continual abuse and most recent assault against my mother. The Policewoman offered some compassionate words and then left to file her report.

Soon after A.P.S. was involved and my 79-year-old mom was informed she had to move. Amanda, Will and I all decided unanimously it would be best if mom moved near me as the 200-mile distance would help mitigate Emily's potential abuse.

Lynn and I worked to find a place for my mom to stay and after about a week when we found a nice, assisted living facility for my mom to stay. Now she did not have to worry about Emily's anger issues and vile language. Mom could now enjoy the company of calm people of her generation. Something she had not been able to do for many years.

While I was teaching a class in Wisconsin for the Army, I was informed about another possible deployment to Kuwait. After I was done teaching the class which lasted about a month. I was sent to the mobilization station in Missouri for screening where I received another multitude of immunizations plus an Anthrax shot. I thought for sure I'd have some reaction, but I had no such problem. The truth is I felt great.

I attended some mobilization training In Arkansas that went on for a couple of months before I was told I was not needed on the mission. I thought just, wow!. This is twice now I was told I was going to the middle east and the rug was pulled out from under me. The reason this time was that the unit going over to Kuwait would have to cross level me or, in other words, lend me from my unit and they did already have another officer with my MOS/AOC in their brigade. So that individual went instead of me. All I could do was throw my hands up in the air. Soon after 2014 came to an end.

In 2015 my wife was mobilized to an air force base in Texas and there she stayed for 10 months. During this time, my mom developed breast cancer, and I had to take her to some of her appointments in Kansas City and other places.

I was now left with two teenagers, a kindergartner and a now 81-year-old woman with cancer to care for as well as work full time to provide income. While Lynn was on active duty, she was an E-6 and made decent money but not enough money to support the family. I still had to work to pay for bills and put food on the table.

I felt I had no choice but to resign from the Army Reserves which I hated to do. I could not perform my duties even one weekend a month as I had no family support locally to take care of my three kids and mom while I was away for reserve duty. I did not want to let the troops down, so I sent my resignation into the Army Reserves. There was also the issue of the false charge of domestic violence against me from my abusive sister and PIG FACE Donald, that I was concerned about. Even though it was expunged the investigators at the security clearance agency in time would find it and could and most likely would not see all the evidence and say that I was simply a wife beater. Which couldn't be further from the truth.

However, the detached FBI agent does not know who I am nor that I was protecting my mother from the same abuse she had received as a wife so she wouldn't have received it as a mother from an abusive sister. But they would never figure it out as they are disconnected and detached from the common man and woman. I have no faith in the humanity of the FBI. One wrong word to them or a mistake taken as a lie and you are a felon. That is an overly aggressive policy to criminalize Americans. Not cool.

So, for the next year I was Mr. Mom. Taking the kids to band practice, football games, plays, and wherever or whenever they needed to go somewhere. Then there was my mom's cancer treatment. She had about

6 rounds of radiation therapy and checkups at the cancer center in K.C. By the time Lynn returned from her mobilization my mom was cancer free, but all the radiation therapy took a huge toll on my mother. I felt so bad for my mom but the best I could do was to hold her hand and offer her support.

Something strange was also starting to happen in my marriage. Lynn could not remember the weekends when I brought the kids to see her, nor could she remember me sending any care packages. I sent six care packages to her by USPS and hand delivered two care packages myself. During this time, I had let myself go and gained about 30 pounds of weight. I now understood and could sympathize with so many Americans who knew better but couldn't do better or wouldn't do better for their health due to their life circumstances. One night in the bedroom after Lynn had returned home, Lynn said somewhere between giddiness and concern Sig you are putting on a belly. I said in reply, I never thought you would notice. Funny, I never commented on how her ass was getting bigger. It was big too. African American men would often come up to her when we were out in public. I had been dealing with that crap for over 25 years. What vibe was she throwing out to attract the brothers. She definitely didn't dress provocatively. I certainly didn't think so as she was often dressed in a frumpy manner.

One day later that Fall, Lynn says to me "Sig, I here there's a chance for a Chaplain Assistant to go to the middle east". I said," Do you really want to go?" To that she nodded her head and said yes. So just a few months later after getting home to her family. She volunteers for another mission again?" I just thought she was patriotic. I might have done the same thing. I did not want to judge.

The day comes a few months later and I'm taking Lynn and the kids to the airport to say goodbye. I didn't realize at the time how profound that goodbye was. She was gone for six months as is the Air Force's deployment length. I believe she was sent to Kuwait for two weeks and then was sent to her Forward Operating Base.

The kids and I would wake up early in the mornings to say goodnight and in the evenings, we would say good morning. We would skype or viber a few times each week. I would inform Lynn of all the things going on with the kids, school and grades, our daughter's graduation I videoed for her and I tried my best to stay on top of everything.

She told stories of all the sorties and bombings the Air Force did in Iraq. Her story of the loss of a female Airman during the loading of munitions was sad and I'm sure it was upsetting for the command at her F.O.B.

The months went by and care package after care package was sent and received. The kids would send letters and our youngest would send seasonal items such as Valentines or Easter Bunny themed kid stuff for her. It seemed as though she enjoyed the packages.

During that time, I got a call from US Army Recruiters to consider coming back in. I began running in the mornings before the kids got up and I started watching what I was eating again. I was getting back in shape. Lynn was due to return in a few months, and I told the recruiter I would meet with him at that time.

In the meantime, my efforts to appeal my case were received and honored by the Governor's Office. All the evidence of my case was presented in context and this time the right audience was listening. I received a complete pardon from the Governor's office. All my rights were restored. I could not have been more relieved. I felt so incredibly fortunate! Blessed

A couple of months passed by, and Lynn returned. I got the kids ready early that morning and went to the airport to pick up my wife of 26 years. I was so looking forward to seeing her again and the kids were very excited. I pulled up to the arriving passengers parking area and got the kids out of the car to go see their mom. Lynn was eager to see them and gave them all a hug. When I went to hug my wife, I got a very odd reception of a halfhearted hug like she was someone I no longer knew. I tried to shake it off that it was probably just her readjustment phase taking place, but it did seem quite off. I took the family out to eat and then we went home.

A week later Lynn did compliment me that I did look good. My effort to get back in the military was paying off physically and I was glad she noticed. I thought maybe things were okay after all. We went to meet the Army recruiter, and he assured me that he had been able to get more Officer'sreappointed than any other recruiter in the region.

I began filling out mounds of paperwork. I submitted and resubmitted documents, DD 214s, Honorable discharges and everything else needed. I met with the Officer in Charge of the recruiting detachment after my recruiter PCS'd. All my documents were submitted to the recruiting battalion, and they told me I was too old! They obviously didn't take in consideration of my previous 15 years of service which is supposed to be subtracted from your actual age for the purpose of qualification at MEPS. Obviously the recruiting command did not realize I was going into the Reserves not active duty. It didn't matter to them I could still run my two miles in under 18:00 minutes. They denied me sight unseen!I was pissed off, frustrated.

Not only was there this issue but a few months previous Lynn had come to visit me in my deer stand behind our property and asked to talk. I thought maybe she wanted to get frisky, but this was not the case. She brought me to our front porch and nervously asked me for a divorce. I was shocked, astounded and insulted. She told me that she was so in love with GOD that she wanted to leave me?!@!This did not compute. God is not a marriage wrecker. I asked her what was really going on. She couldn't or wouldn't tell me.

We went to marriage counseling at my insistence. I was not going to let that woman that had returned from overseas ruin my kids' lives and ruin our marriage of 26 years. I felt so shit upon by her. I had taken care of the kids, my mom, all of her things for nearly two years while she was gone and when she returned, she asked for a divorce. She couldn't have been more ungrateful. Talk about disrespect and insult. That was pretty close to a 10 on the disrespect scale.

She took on a new job in sales and this lasted for about 10 months. Every day she came home acting miserable most days, griping about her boss, and griping about all the driving she had to do. She was just miserable. She was so miserable that I began looking for another job out of the area that we were living in.

In the Spring of the next year, I received two job offers. One was in the Midland-Odessa area of Texas the other job was working with the Navajo Nation in Arizona. Lynn seemed happy that we would be leaving the area so I continued to pursue both job offers. I did a background check for both government jobs and I passed. I felt relieved.

We tried selling the house and we decided to head to Arizona. We had discussed the possibilities of both locations to family friends. We were encouraged to seek out the job in Arizona. The environment of Midland-Odessa is well known for its oil fields and was thought not to be as good an environment for our youngest child. We decided that Arizona would be a better situation for our family and youngest son who was now 9 years old.

As soon as I received the job offer in Arizona Lynn wasted no time packing and we visited real estate agents to make sure the house sold. We had two separate yard sales and had some success our "excess" household goods. I remembered helping my in-laws in upstate NY pack up from their home of 30 years.

They had mound after mound of old stuff either to be sold or scrapped. They had even contracted out their very own waste dumpster.

While we were boxing items, rearranging, compressing, and selling things I had flashbacks to what my in-laws had experienced. Though our little family had only been at our residence for about 12 years at that point moving day came. If it couldn't fit onto the truck it wasn't going. I'm sure many can relate.

We ended up getting an additional U-Haul trailer and all of America knows the rest of the story. We made our way into the four corners area with the movers right behind us. When we got to our destination, we were told housing was not ready for us. Lynn was having a conniption fit as she was concerned about the movers having our stuff and needing to leave for another move.

To me it was not unlike any military move with not all the ducks being lined up in a row on our arrival. The house or domicile we were supposed to move into was not quite ready as I had anticipated. We were provided temporary housing with all our possessions moved into the domicile we were to stay in. I had no problem with the provision, but Lynn was less than pleased and made our 18-year-old daughter Grace upset and anxious. Our young 9-year-old son had no such anxiety.

In the next two weeks, I had finished orientation at the new hospital, my mini me Joe had started his school year and Grace was headed back home on a flight to Kansas. We eventually settled into our assigned bungalow and life slowly began to normalize. We began meeting our neighbors and I began to get to know my coworkers who mostly seemed to be 15-20 years younger than me. My age was catching up to me or maybe vice versa.

I eventually found out I was working with some fellow veterans, uniformed health service officers, former Peace Corps members and many recent college graduates. It was quite the eclectic group of workers but overall, it was a very functional hospital that was not as efficient as it could have been as it was reliant on government funds solely to operate.

Lynn, Joe and I would go out on little trips on weekends when we had no other obligations and began to appreciate the beauty of the landscape that was so starkly different from where we had come from. For her part, Lynn had renewed a boy scout pack that had not existed for over 10 years in the service unit of the Navajo Nation that we were in. We managed to get about 25 young scouts in Joe's pack that year. It was a mutually beneficial arrangement, a win-win for the Navajo youth and our boy.

It was during this time of scouting that Lynn would be gone a couple nights of the week for scouting purposes. This lasted for several months. I didn't think much of it as she said she was helping other Tribes start scouting packs. She had previously worked for the organization back home, so I thought it was just what she had to do to maintain her job.

We also found out that our home still had not sold after 5 months on the market. So, our 19 year old daughter moved in with some friends and began renting the house from us. This was a great help but also a potential nightmare for home repairs. I'm sure any homeowning parent can empathize.

Little Joe began school and immediately was picked on by his Navajo classmates for no other reason than being different "white". Joe experienced bullying for two weeks. His teacher at the time was new and was unable to control the class and could be observed crying at times. Not a good environment for any of them. We soon pulled Little Joe out of that school and transferred him to the neighboring elementary. At this new elementary school, he did much better. Classes were well organized and controlled. It all made sense when I found out that his new teacher was a Veteran of the Army. Accountability has its benefits at all ages and for all ethnicities.

The remainder of the school year was as it should have been. Regular meetings with the teacher regarding student progress took place. Mr. B did a great job with the students and what he was given by the school district. I felt little Joe was fortunate to have him.

Oddly enough at the end of the school year we found out that Mr. B was going to be leaving. I could only think how unfortunate for the school and the students he could have positively impacted. I often wonder about the wisdom of school districts. What parent doesn't?

A few months later and the school year was now over, and I was counting down the days until my contract was up. My house payment hadn't stopped and as luck would have it my old job was again available as the replacement they had found for me was found out to be an overly dramatic ill-fittingemployee.

Not terribly unlike a sociopathic fellow government employee that was a good incentive to leave as well as she made the entire department less happy, less functional and added unnecessary drama. I received a positive review for my time in my GS- 11 position and was glad to be leaving on a positive note.

CHAPTER 16

A New Chapter

In July of 2019 we returned to Kansas. It was a typical U-Haul cross country move again. I was happy to return to my home state but my spouse, not so much. In August after our return, Lynn began looking for employment in the area. She tried several radio stations, but nothing stuck for her. Then one morning, she just acted limp and lifeless. I asked her what was wrong and she asked me if I wanted a sexless marriage? To which I replied no, as any normal man might reply. Then she stated that she wanted to file for divorce. At this point, I did not offer resistance and decided to let her go.

This was a very trying time for me. I had been married for 28 years almost 29 and I was losing my long time friend and confidant. We had been through so much together through my mobilizations and hers as well and I felt we had been mostly supportive of one another. I soon learned that none of that mattered in the here and now.

I waited through September when "The talk" happened and I still had not received any divorce papers. While she was working on completing paperwork for her position as an instructor for the National Guard in Alabama, I asked her what the holdup was? She then shouted at me," that she had not had time to follow up on the process." I then shouted back at her, "why hadn't she made the time since she wanted the divorce so badly."

On October 3rd I received the notice that Lynn had filed for divorce.

All I could think is that we were now just going to become another statistic for the failure of the institution of marriage in our increasingly self-gratuitous and narcissistic society.

Due to the fact that so many millions of couples have divorced prior to our divorce, we were able to benefit from an expedited on-line divorce. We initially appeared in court on Friday the 13th. I thought, "how fitting". I had all my documents in hand, and I had agreed to all of my soon to be ex-wife's demands most of which had to do with walking away with $20,000 and being guaranteed another $60,000.00 in 10 years' time. Wouldn't you know, the one who wanted the divorce so badly (Lynn) had actually, left her copy of the petition for divorce at her apartment (She was always scatterbrained). I had my copy of the divorce petition and other documents but without her copy for some reason it was delayed until the following Tuesday.

That following Tuesday came, and we attended our divorce hearing. By 10:30 that morning, it was finalized. For the first time in 28 years, I was not bound to someone to support, care for, provide for and love. I couldn't understand it and would have never predicted how the flood of emotions came over me.

Tears began streaming and I just felt stupefied and so bad for our 10-year-old son who would now be back and forth between states every other year. I got myself together and went back to work to continue being the man I was and am and to get my mind off of what had just happened.

Even though the divorce process went relatively smooth for us I couldn't help but feel that I'd just been raked over the coals of the US. Divorce Court System. What did she have to suffer?

She received $20,000 up front and I was paying her another $60,000.00 over the next ten years. How was she suffering? She got her tour in Alabama with the National Guard for four years as an E7, making equivalent pay to mine in the civilian sector and she took our son with her.

I now have loads of empathy and sympathy for other divorced men.

The Divorce Court System needs some serious updating in this "equivalent society" of ours. You see men and women are not equals but will always be opposites by law of nature, no matter how badly the court system and society continue to bastardize this reality.

In the next few weeks, I went back and forth with my recruiter preparing paperwork for the Board of the Army Reserves so my Recruiter could send my packet to Ft. Knox Human Resource Command. In November, my packet was sent to the board, and I would have to await the results in the next few months.

The results were supposed to be posted in January but were delayed due to the dreaded COVID-19 SARS- COV 2 virus. I did not receive my results until four months later. The US Army apparently needed me back and approved my rank to be restored!I couldn't believe it and was beside myself in joy!

The divorce court couldn't take that away from me. But if I wasn't careful the security clearance people could. I continued to pay the civil court sanctioned extortion to my ex-wife and pay my bills and kept my nose clean.

Right before Lynn left for Alabama, she did an act of total disregard and dereliction of maternal court sanctioned duty. She had let her Tricare coverage lapse because she didn't want to pay the $700.00 back pay to provide Tricare coverage for the kids. As bad luck would have it, our oldest son got in a wreck delivering pizzas. He was sent to the hospital for checkup and was cleared for discharge with nothing told to me about how that ER visit was billed and who it was billed to.

Fast forward two months and my oldest son is living with me due to his college being closed due to the COVID 19 virus. He comes home after getting off his shift at work and tells me he's had really bad pains in his bowels for a couple days. So, I took Tom to the local minor emergency clinic and there they informed me that he was not covered by Tricare and my bill for that visit was $3500.

A month after that, I get a bill in the mail from a claims company because my ex-wife had named me as the guarantor for my son's medical insurance when she knew full well per the agreement in the divorce she was responsible for the medical costs due to the fact she would be on Tricare. She knew I was paying their optical and dental insurance and decided to stick me with a $3700 E.R. bill from Tom's car wreck when he was delivering pizza.

On a security clearance investigation, they will investigate…

(1) Guideline A: Allegiance to the United States

This is rarely the cause of a clearance denial or revocation, but <u>political dissidents beware</u>. You can certainly participate in politics but defamatory speech against the government is not looked upon well. The next time someone talks to you about overthrowing the government, you certainly don't want to lend them your ear.

(2) Guideline B: Foreign Influence

Foreign influence is an increasingly significant factor in security clearance determinations, both for naturalized citizens and for those whose parents were born in a foreign country. Your security clearance investigation will seek to ensure that <u>you don't have divided loyalties</u>. SEAD 4 does clarify that dual citizenship is not a disqualifier for a security clearance, but dual citizens should not be taking advantage of their foreign citizenship.

(3) Guideline C: Foreign Preference

<u>Foreign preference</u> – very similar to foreign influence, also comes down to loyalty. It is frequently cited as a factor for dual citizens. If you're a dual citizen you'll want to avoid taking advantage of the benefits of that citizenship – including traveling on a foreign passport.

(4) Guideline D: Sexual Behavior

Sexual behavior is rarely used for a clearance denial or revocation. When it is, it typically relates to criminal sexual behavior or an extramarital affair. Even an extramarital affair is <u>not likely to result in a clearance denial</u>. But if you haven't disclosed that indiscretion and would go to great lengths to hide it, the risk for a foreign government is a consideration.

(5) Guideline E: Personal Conduct

Personal conduct is a common disqualifying condition, and it is most frequently used against applicants who have <u>lied on their SF-86</u>. Fabricating details on your security clearance application is a sure sign of dishonesty. That's why the rule about the <u>SF-86</u> is to always be truthful. Don't disclose unnecessary information, but omitting a known drug use (which may or may not be a disqualifying issue) is certain to come back to haunt you.

(6) Guideline F: Financial Considerations

<u>Financial considerations</u> are the number one clearance killer. The idea is, if you can't be responsible for your finances, than you may not be trustworthy with classified information, either. Not all debt is considered equally – medical debt, debt due to lay-offs and other explained debt can be mitigated. A problem with overspending is not as favorable and puts you at risk for foreign espionage efforts and the chance for a quick pay off.

(7) Guideline G: Alcohol Consumption

This adjudicative guideline comes down to <u>alcohol abuse</u> – not the regular glass of wine before dinner or the occasional bender. It is often seen through repeated citations for Driving Under the Influence (DUI) or public intoxication. If you've been cited recently – or frequently – for alcohol related offenses, consider enrolling yourself in an alcohol education course.

(8) Guideline H: Drug Involvement and Substance Misuse

Drug involvement frequently gives <u>young security-clearance applicants sweaty palms</u>. But infrequent drug use can be mitigated – particularly with the passage of time. Even a habitual drug user can show that he's changed his ways with the passage of time. So be honest on your application but avoid any contact with drugs in the future.

(9) Guideline I: Psychological Conditions

<u>Mental health</u> is one of the more controversial adjudicative criteria. In recent years the guideline has been updated to clarify that seeking mental health counseling is not a disqualifying factor for a security clearance. The issue for the government is untreated mental illness, unreliability or dysfunctional behavior. If you have received medical counseling for anything other than a spousal, family issue, or military service-related issue, you will be asked to provide an "Authorization of Release of Medical Information" which allows your medical provider to answer three questions related to your judgement, reliability and prognosis.

(10) Guideline J: Criminal Conduct

Criminal offenses are considered based on three categories – felonies, misdemeanors and infractions. <u>All must be reported</u> on the SF-86. When in doubt as to whether or not you were actually arrested for that college drinking incident (a common issue), go ahead and include that information on your SF-86 – along with mitigating factors such as a character reference.

(11) Guideline K: Handling Protected Information

This criteria is more often used to revoke an existing clearance and comes down to the ability to responsibly carry out your duties in <u>handling classified information</u>. Repeatedly failing to lock a safe, for instance, may be seen as a callous attitude toward your duties, and could result in a clearance revocation if the situation is serious.

(12) Guideline L: Outside Activities

This criteria often <u>comes down to relationships</u> – particularly financial ones – with a foreign country. If you're currently being paid by a foreign company or government for any reason, cease that relationship and be sure you can clearly explain your involvement on your SF-86.

(13) Guideline M: Use of Information Technology Systems

From: TheBalanceCareers.com

Relating to item 6; I have been paying off this bill now for a couple of months as well as forking over the$250 monthly on top of the $20,000.00 initial down payment for the divorce settlement. So, you see divorce is like a second mortgage but with nothing to show for it but lost money which compounds monthly. It's no wonder why after experiences like mine, men are embarking on the MGTOW (Men Going Their Own Way) or Red Pill philosophy. What person in their right mind would want to experience the heart break of a breakup and financial loss repeatedly. Men are starting to wake up to the lie that society has been conditioning them into as being the foot stool for all that a woman desires. Being Monk like may not be so bad. It is actually becoming "trendy".

It's anybody's guess what the security clearance investigators will say regarding any of the above factors. But being that I'm a white conservative heterosexual Christian male, I may be at a disadvantage, but at least I can say the board did select me. I passed my physical at an MTF (Military Treatment Facility) which my ex taunted me that I would not. (SMH) We all know life is unfair and it very well could be the security clearance investigators say no, or I could get lucky, and I'll be a Major once again.

I've done nothing wrong in the past ten years other than pay my bills, provide for my family and care for the people around me and become extremely opinionated about women and their cat like and often self-destructive behavior. What I have found to be really ironic is that many women are their own worst enemies and become their very own homewreckers. Yes, men can exhibit the same behavior. However, the majority of divorces are filed by women to the tune of 80% and it jumps up to 90% among college educated women. So, it cannot be disputed that women lead men 4 to 1 in home wrecking! (American Sociological Association 2015) You go girl!!

If I were a civilian contractor, the process would have only taken 90 days but due to being in the military it takes on average 6-8 months and that was before the "pandemic". Just ask any military recruiter, Soldier, Sailor or Marine that the "pandemic" has thrown everything off course, especially with new recruits, field training to battle assembly for Reservists. It has affected the military in ways not unlike the civilian sector but in other ways the civilian sector can't imagine. Everything but the utmost urgent military training and operations is either on hold or delayed. Can you imagine being overseas and having the resupply of necessary items delayed for weeks or a month. Believe it, it is now history and current events that our nation is reeling from.

It has now been four years since my divorce. My ex-wife (The Chaplain Assistant) is remarried and married quickly three years after our divorce and is now on Active Duty with the Air National Guard. I had my 12-year-old back for a year. Now he has been back with his mother for three years and I have only seen him for two weeks in the summer and Christmas time. I too am now remarried to whom is a far better match and has been through her own set of desperate situations. Fate is a funny thing. I now know how shallow and vapid so many women can be, and I do believe in toxic femininity. It is very much a real thing.

I'm now back in the Army Reserves and have passed every ACFT given and will continue to do so. I will always try to have a positive impact on fellow service members. They are the most precious gift our nation has to give to benefit our people and the world.

It seems my two sons are very proud of their father and keep in contact with me frequently. I too am very proud of them and their unlimited potential.

I pray to God for our nation daily. I pray it does not tear itself apart in the same fashion as it has enabled so many families to do. A house divided will not stand!

CHAPTER 17

Introspection and Reflection

It is now 2024 and throughout my whole life which was impacted by my father's mental illness which has indelibly impacted my behavior and how I treat people not as in the manner of my father; the status of treatment for the mentally ill has improved from a pharmaceutical perspective but from a human to human perspective it has declined and declined in a manner that is dangerous for society.

We have seen pandering from political "leaders" if you choose to call them that, which has done very little to help the plight of the mentally ill nor the family members impacted by the mentally ill family member. Here I sight our health systems apathetic and vapid approach to mental illness and the decrease in health care capacity for the mentally ill.

The lack of psychiatric inpatient beds is a huge national issue. There has been a decrease of over 500,000 beds since the 1950s when our population was only 152 million people. Today our population is double that and our number of citizens with mental illness and drug usage has skyrocketed since that time.

VA (Veterans Affairs), Department of Defense Medical Centers and psychiatric inpatient units within prisons and penitentiaries do provide beds for the mentally ill. However, these beds are NOT for the general public.

This is a huge disservice to the American public. Big Pharma of all should be contributing to find a solution but that is like asking Al Sharpton to assist the Anti-Defamation League.

Daily in meetings, I hear multiple times of how patients with psychiatric issues must remain hospitalized for days on end because an appropriate psychiatric facility bed can't be found in the Kansas City or surrounding area. How could this be if our medical system is so great. Though, don't believe for a minute that Universal Health Coverage is the answer.

The Navajo as well as all Native American Tribes have endowed upon them by charter and treaty, Universal Health Coverage. Not once in my entire time working with the Navajo, did I ever run across a long-term inpatient psychiatric treatment facility for the Navajo nor a psychiatrist for the Navajo service unit I was working at nor the Navajo Nation as a whole. The Navajo and all other Tribes deserve the benefit of long- term psychiatric services just as any U.S citizen may be entitled to. Yet they exist only in scarcity.

The only hope for the mentally ill and health care providers is if CMS/ Medicare/ Medicaid change the weight of the DRGs (Diagnostic Related Groupings) for different mental illness and mental illness is treated in the same manner as we treat diseases of different organ systems of the body. It is wholly inconsistent that we don't treat them the same especially considering how JCAHO (Joint Commission for Accreditation of Health Care Organizations) stresses the importance of continuity of care.

My hope for this book is it would be a story of resiliency and the spirit of hope that a human is capable of having. I do feel by and large this story is about those qualities. It is my hope that many people can relate to the moderate success I have had in my life despite all the abuse and misdeeds I suffered along with my siblings and especially my brother that I witnessed what he had suffered, and it was far from the way a son should be raised by his father. For my part, the abuse I experienced firsthand; I can only try and frame it objectively after 36 years being removed from it. Again, it was a far cry from the way a father should rear a child. My mother did the best she could under some terrible circumstances and managed to keep the family together and maintain her teaching profession. At my mother's funeral (her death was COVID 19 related) my brother and I marveled at my mother's feat, and we determined that about 95% of women in today's world would have just thrown up their hands and left my dad. However, our mom did not leave our father, and I can no doubt thank her for the strength she provided me to make it through some tough situations and even achieve a few things that some people had doubts I would achieve. When other people give up on you such as an ex-wife. Don't give up on yourself and always have faith in God.

For the record, Lynn nor any of the women I have dated since would have not lasted a month in the household I was brought up in. They would have left at the first sight of conflict. It is likely a blessing and God's will that she and I parted ways. As in most things, a better perspective of a situation can be seen from a greater distance and not so when so close in proximity.

Another parting insight was provided to me by a coworker who was a former Full Bird Colonel that she had received from another Full Bird Colonel. It is a scenario allegedly from Chinese military leaders not unlike those thought out by the teachers and cadre at the Army War College that if true could be implication for war with China. You can make your own decision about what may or may not be happening in our nation in our recent history and current events. It can be read on the following pages.

The Woohoo from Wuhan!

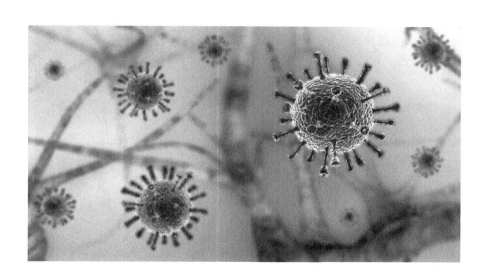

December, 2005

3-1-9

The following is the actual text of a speech delivered in December 2005 by Comrade Chi Haotian the Vice-Chairman of China's Military Commission to top officers and generals. Keep in mind that China has for many years advocated deceitful and covert warfare against its enemies. This is their Modus Operandi. There should be little question that a "Bird Flu" Pandemic would deeply excite them. (Don't forget how they have poisoned thousands of American pets and knowingly placed lead paints on toddler's toys.)

"Comrades, I'm very excited today, because the large-scale online survey sina.com that was done for us showed that our next generation is quite promising and our Party's cause will be carried on. In answering the question, "Will you shoot at women, children and prisoners of war," more than 80 per cent of the respondents answered in the affirmative, exceeding by far our expectations. Today I'd like to focus on why we asked sina. com to conduct this online survey among our people. My speech today is a sequel to my speech last time, during which I started with a discussion of the issue of the three islands [Taiwan, Diaoyu Islands and the Spratley Islands --- Ott] and mentioned that 20 years of the idyllic theme of 'peace and development' had come to an end and concluded that modernization under the saber is the only option for China's next phase. I also mentioned we have a vital stake overseas. The central issue of this survey appears to be whether one should shoot at women, children and prisoners of war, but its real significance goes far beyond that. Ostensibly, our intention is mainly to figure out what the Chinese people's attitude towards war is: If these future soldiers do not hesitate to kill even noncombatants, they'll naturally be doubly ready and ruthless in killing combatants. Therefore, the responses to the survey questions may reflect the general attitude people have towards war. We wanted to know: If China's global development will necessitate massive deaths in enemy countries; will our people endorse that scenario? Will they be for or against it?

The fact is, our 'development' refers to the great revitalization of the Chinese nation, which, of course, is not limited to the land we have now but also includes the whole world. As everybody knows, according to the views propagated by the Western scholars, humanity as a whole originated from one single mother in Africa. Therefore, no race can claim racial superiority. However, according to the research conducted by most Chinese scholars, the Chinese are different from other races on earth. We did not originate in Africa. Instead, we originated independently in the land of China. Therefore, we can rightfully assert that we are the product of cultural roots of more than a million years, civilization and progress of more than ten thousand years, an ancient nation of five thousand years, and a single Chinese entity of two thousand years. This is the Chinese nation that calls itself 'descendants of Yan and Huang.'

During our long history, our people have disseminated throughout the Americas and the regions along the Pacific Rim, and they became Indians in the Americas and the East Asian ethnic groups in the South Pacific. We all know that on account of our national superiority, during the thriving and prosperous Tang Dynasty our civilization was at the peak of the world. We were the center of the world civilization, and no other civilization in the world was comparable to ours. Later on, because of our complacency, narrow-mindedness, and the self-enclosure of our own country, we were surpassed by Western civilization, and the center of the world shifted to the West.

In reviewing history, one may ask: Will the center of the world civilization shift back to China? Actually, Comrade Liu Huaqing made similar points in the early 1980's Based on an historical analysis, he pointed out that the center of world civilization is shifting. It shifted from the East to Western Europe and later to the United States; now it is shifting back to the East. Therefore, if we refer to the 19th Century as the British Century and the 20th century as the American Century, then the 21st Century will be the Chinese Century! (Wild applause fills the auditorium.)

Our Chinese people are wiser than the Germans because, fundamentally, our race is superior to theirs. As a result, we have a longer history, more people, and larger land area. On this basis, our ancestors left us with the two most essential heritages, which are atheism and great unity. It was Confucius, the founder of our Chinese culture, who gave us these heritages. These two heritages determined that we have a stronger ability to survive than the West. That is why the Chinese race has been able to prosper for so long. We are destined 'not to be buried by either heaven or earth' no matter how severe the natural, man-made, and national disasters. This is our advantage. Take response to war as an example. The reason that the United States remains today is that it has never seen war on its mainland. Once its enemies aim at the mainland, the enemies would have already reached Washington before its congress finishes debating and authorizes the president to declare war. But for us, we don't waste time on these trivial things. Maybe you have now come to understand why we recently decided to further promulgate atheism. If we let theology from the West into China and empty us from the inside, if we let all Chinese people listen to God and follow God, who will obediently listen to us and follow us? If the common people don't believe Comrade Hu Jintao is a qualified leader, begin to question his authority, and want to monitor him, if the religious followers in our society question why we are leading God in churches, can our Party continue to rule China?

The first pressing issue facing us is living space. This is the biggest focus of the revitalization of the Chinese race. In my last speech, I said that the fight over basic living resources (including land and ocean) is the source of the vast majority of wars in history. This may change in the information age, but not fundamentally. Our per capita resources are much less than those of Germany's back then. In addition, economic development in the last twenty-plus years had a negative impact, and climates are rapidly changing for the worse. Our resources are in very short supply. The environment is severely polluted, especially that of soil, water, and air. Not only our ability to sustain and develop our race, but even its survival is gravely threatened, to a degree much greater than faced Germany back then. Anybody who has been to Western countries knows that their living space is much better than ours. They have forests alongside the highways, while we hardly have any trees on our streets. Their sky is often blue with white clouds, while our sky is covered with a layer of dark haze. Their tap water is clean enough for drinking, while even our ground water is so polluted that it can't be drunk without filtering. They have few people in the streets, and two or three people can occupy a small residential building; in contrast our streets are always crawling with people, and several people have to share one room.

Many years ago, there was a book titled Yellow Catastrophes. It said that, due to our following the American style of consumption, our limited resources would no longer support the population and society would collapse once our population reaches 1.3 billion. Now our population has already exceeded this limit, and we are now relying on imports to sustain our nation. It's not that we haven't paid attention to this issue. The Ministry of Land Resources is specialized in this issue. But we must understand that the term 'living space' (lebensraum) is too closely related to Nazi Germany.

The reason we don't want to discuss this too openly is to avoid the West's association of us with Nazi Germany, which could in turn reinforce the view that China is a threat. Therefore, in our emphasis on He Xin's new theory, 'Human Rights are just living rights' we only talk about 'living' but not 'space' so as to avoid using the term 'living space.' From the perspective of history, the reason that China is faced with the issue of living space is because Western countries have developed ahead of Eastern countries. Western countries established colonies all around the world, therefore giving themselves an advantage on the issue of living space. To solve this problem, we must lead the Chinese people outside of China, so that they can develop outside of China.

Would the United States allow us to go out to gain new living space? First, if the United States is firm in blocking us, it is hard for us to do anything significant to Taiwan and some other countries! Second, even if we could snatch some land from Taiwan, Vietnam, India, or even Japan, how much more living space can we get? Very trivial! Only countries like the United States, Canada and Australia have the vast land to serve our need for mass colonization.

Therefore, solving the 'issue of America' is the key to solving all other issues. First, this makes it possible for us to have many people migrate there and even establish another China under the same leadership of the CCP. America was originally discovered by the ancestors of the yellow race, but Columbus gave credit to the White race. We the descendants of the Chinese nation are ENTITLED to the possession of the land! It is historical destiny that China and United States will come into unavoidable confrontation on a narrow path and fight. In the long run, the relationship of China and the United States is one of a life-and-death struggle. Of course, right now it is not the time to openly break up with them yet. Our reform and opening to the outside world still rely on their capital and technology. We still need America. Therefore, we must do everything we can to promote our relationship with America, learn from America in all aspects and use America as an example to reconstruct our country. Only by using special means to 'clean up' America will we be able to lead the Chinese people there. Only by using non-destructive weapons that can kill many people will we be able to reserve America for ourselves.

There has been rapid development of modern biological technology, and new bioweapons have been invented one after another. Of course we have not been idle; in the past years we have seized the opportunity to master weapons of this kind. We are capable of achieving our purpose of 'cleaning up' America all of a sudden. When Comrade Xiaoping was still with us, the Party Central Committee had the perspicacity to make the right decision not to develop aircraft carrier groups and focused instead on developing lethal weapons that can eliminate mass populations of the enemy country. Biological weapons are unprecedented in their ruthlessness, but if the Americans do not die then the Chinese have to die. If the Chinese people are strapped to the present land, a total societal collapse is bound to take place. According to the computations of the author of Yellow Peril, more than half of the Chinese will die, and that figure would be more than 800 million people! Just after the liberation, our yellow land supported nearly 500 million people, while today the official figure of the population is more than 1.3 billion. This yellow land has reached the limit of its capacity. One day, who know how soon it will come, the great collapse will occur any time and more than half of the population will have to go.

It is indeed brutal to kill one or two hundred million Americans. But that is the only path that will secure a Chinese century, a century in which the CCP leads the world. We, as revolutionary humanitarians, do not want deaths, but if history confronts us with a choice between deaths of Chinese and those of Americans, we'd have to pick the latter, as, for us, it is more important to safeguard the lives of the Chinese people and the life of our Party. The last problem I want to talk about is that of firmly seizing the preparations for military battle. The central committee believes, as long as we resolve the United States problem at one blow, our domestic problems will all be readily solved. Therefore, our military battle preparation appears to aim at Taiwan, but in fact is aimed at the United States, and the preparation is far beyond the scope of attacking aircraft carriers or satellites. Marxism pointed out that violence is the midwife for the birth of the new society. Therefore, war is the midwife for the birth of China's century."

Very respectfully signing out,
S. Magnusson

Printed in the United States
by Baker & Taylor Publisher Services